P9-CML-953

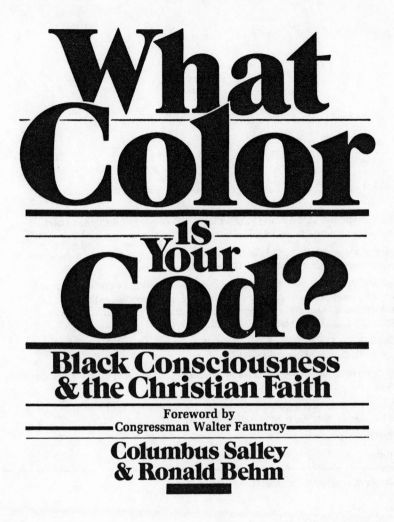

What Color is Your God?

Black Consciousness & the Christian Faith

Foreword by
Congressman Walter Fauntroy

Columbus Salley
& Ronald Behm

InterVarsity Press
Downers Grove
Illinois 60515

InterVarsity Press is the book-publishing division of Inter-Varsity Christian Fellowship, a student movement active on campus at hundreds of universities, colleges and schools of nursing. For information about local and regional activities, write IVCF, 233 Langdon St., Madison, WI 53703.

Distributed in Canada through InterVarsity Press, 1875 Leslie St., Unit 10, Don Mills, Ontario M3B 2M5, Canada.

All Scripture quotations are from the Revised Standard Version of the Bible, copyrighted 1946, 1952 © 1971, 1973.

Quotations from Stokely Carmichael and Charles Hamilton, Black Power: The Politics of Liberation © 1967 are used by permission of Random House.

ISBN 0-87784-791-6

Printed in the United States of America

Library of Congress Cataloging in Publication Data

Salley, Columbus.
 What color is your God?

   Previous ed. published in 1970 as: Your God is too white.
   Includes bibliographical references and index.
   1. Race (Theology)   I. Behm, Ronald.   II. Title.
III. Title: Black consciousness and the Christian
faith.
BT734.2.S25   1981   261.8'348   81-6758
ISBN 0-87784-791-6   AACR2

---

17   16   15   14   13   12   11   10   9   8   7   6   5   4   3   2   1
95   94   93   92   91   90   89   88   87   86   85   84   83   82   81

To my *wife*, Maria, and to my children, Jennifer and Christopher, *my present and future.*
To my *beautiful Black mother, Vurnetha Donley, who kept me alive.*
And to *Black people everywhere who bought me, nourished me and paid for me.*
Columbus Salley

To my *wife*, Barbara, and to our children: Herschel and Kurtis Jackson, Ronda Jean and Matthew Samuel Behm.
Ronald Behm

Acknowledgments

We would like to acknowledge Congressman Walter Fauntroy for having taken time out of his very busy schedule to write the Foreword.

And special thanks go to Joan Guest of InterVarsity Press for having made it possible for us to get together again to revise what we believe will be a very important book.

Foreword

We are living in a period when history is very close to repeating itself with respect to religious intolerance and distortion and misapplication of Christian principles.

At the height of American slavery in the early and mid-nineteenth century the Bible and Christianity were the tools of White plantation owners to oppress and suppress the legitimate human aspirations of Black slaves. The Whites hypocritically preached that God and Christ supported the subjugation of a group of people because of the color of their skin.

Today the religious hypocrisy has taken on a different form and sophistication. It no longer directly and forthrightly argues a perverted Christian doctrine of White superiority and Black inferiority. Instead, the new hypocrisy lambastes those who support abortion, while lauding reductions in food stamps that feed hungry children; it clamors for private, church-supported schools, while condemning federal aid to public schools—the primary educational hope for poor and disadvantaged youngsters; it espouses the virtues of family life, but eschews support for programs which help the elderly, the homeless and jobless.

This new religious hypocrisy mounts its charge in contravention to our Lord's inaugural address: "The Spirit of the Lord is upon me, because he has anointed me to preach good news to the poor. He has sent me to proclaim release to the captives and recovering of sight to the blind, to set at liberty those who are oppressed" (Lk 4:18).

This religious hypocrisy is important to note because it is part of a growing trend in America that incorrectly and naively purports that American racism is almost dead and therefore there is little or no prejudice against Blacks, Hispanics, Asians or poor people because of their race or social standing. And it is dangerous, because it has persuaded well-meaning Christians to support its narrow, selfish point of view.

This leads me to Columbus Salley and Ronald Behm and their work, *What Color Is Your God?* Their book is more than a commentary on racism and Christianity in America. It is a well-documented history of the root causes of distorted perceptions of what Christianity means for Blacks and Whites in this country.

Dr. Salley and Rev. Behm carefully expose the abomination of White misrepresentations of Christianity during slavery and factually argue that Christianity is colorblind: "Color distinctions to justify one man's dominance over another man are basically the fruits of racist minds. God as revealed in the Bible is not governed by distinctions of color."

The authors further enforce the fundamental concept that the Christian religion is raceless, that "we are one in Christ," by noting that "the most obvious application of biblical teaching concerning the creation of man is that all people have equal value and dignity."

Such words are not only encouraging for us as Christians,

but should help remind us as Americans of our nation's avowed commitment to equality as embodied in the Constitution.

Furthermore, Salley and Behm, perhaps most importantly, offer very concrete ideas about how we can begin to resolve the American race problem, at least among those of us who call ourselves Christians, particularly our White brothers and sisters. They suggest: "Christians may provide leadership to programs which seek to promote racial justice and harmony: for example, educating Whites in the larger society at all levels concerning the need for social and attitudinal change."

These are some of the reasons that, for me, *What Color Is Your God?* is more than an intellectual exercise or academic analytical essay. It can be a useful tool in educating Blacks and Whites about the historical distortions of Christianity and how these have had a negative impact on race relations in this country. It is hope for some and encouragement for most Blacks who understand that Christianity transcends race and is not a "White man's religion." Finally, Salley and Behm give us spiritual food to nourish our wills so that we will not be blinded by hypocritical rhetoric but will act to educate all Christians, Whites especially, about the whole gospel, and with that we can begin to live the great commandment of our Lord Jesus, "Thou shalt love thy neighbor as thyself."

Walter E. Fauntroy
Washington, D.C.
July 1981

Congressman Fauntroy is the Congressional representative for the District of Columbia and chairman of the Congressional Black Caucus. A Democrat, he is also pastor of the New Bethel Baptist Church in Washington, D.C.

Introduction: Where Are We Today?

The turbulent era of the Civil Rights Movement of the sixties almost seems like ancient history. The names Rap Brown, Stokely Carmichael, Floyd McKissick, Bull Connors, Huey Newton, Angela Davis and George Wallace are almost forgotten. The struggles, the tears and even the sacrificed lives are barely remembered—tragically forgotten by White and Black Americans. We seem to persist in this malady of erasing our history.

White America has largely settled down to business as usual because Black protest has apparently diminished or diffused. Seemingly, much progress has been made. The Civil Rights Laws prohibit racial discrimination from the Federal government on down in education, employment and housing. Black persons have been elected to political positions in greater numbers than ever before. Some Blacks have moved to the suburbs. Black persons are seen on TV shows and commercials as participants in the "Pepsi generation," as consumers and users of Dial soap, Dristan, Excedrin. In fact, some evidence exists that America has been "blackenized" (at least superficially) through the popularity of Black music, sports, hairstyles and cultural expressions.

But has the victory for full visibility and equality been won? Having passed through the seventies—that period of "benign neglect"—what substantial gains have accrued to the Black community? Are we as a nation less divided, less unequal, less racist, less discriminatory than we were when the landmark Kerner Report (and who even remembers that name today?) declared us "two nations, separate and un-equal"? Does that "explosive mixture" which is created by White racism still brew in the ghettoes of our urban centers?

Still Relevant

Having documented our perspectives on these and other questions almost eleven years ago in *Your God Is Too White*, we must conclude today that very little has changed in White-racist America vis-à-vis Blacks, and that we are now at the explosion point prophesied in the Kerner Report of 1968. These realities make it even more imperative that we make good on the challenge issued by Ed Riddick in the foreword to *Your God Is Too White*. He challenged White Christians to "take the crosses from their necks and their rostrum de-signs and put them on their backs in a common struggle to make this fractured nation a human community."

Some would say that our observations are hyperbolic in light of the progress made by Blacks and Whites during the last decade. But we would respond by agreeing with a state-ment from the National Conference of the Black Theology Project in Atlanta in 1977:

We do not believe that better jobs and bigger houses, color televisions and late-model cars prove that people have at-tained the abundant life of which Jesus spoke. That abundant life cannot be experienced by a people ca̲ idolatry of a sensate and materialistic culture. . . . Com ment to physical gratification as the purpose of life and voidance of the gospel's moral, ethical standards provide false foundations for hard choices. Such false values divide and separate a people who would be free.[1]

We believe now, as we did more than a decade ago, that collective and constructive actions by Blacks and Whites, Christian and non-Christian, can help solve the personal and social problems related to racism in America.

We still believe that Christianity, if viewed apart from its White-racist expression, is a truly revolutionary force which meets the individual needs of Blacks (and others) who ultimately must face the true God who has made himself known in Jesus Christ. Thus, in the following pages, we intend to go beyond the question of racism to the question of the Black person's responsibility to view Christianity independently of White-racist definitions and institutional expressions.

We still believe that the pervasive perception among Blacks of the Whiteness of God and Jesus is the major barrier to their experiencing Christianity as a force which liberates and humanizes rather than oppresses, exploits and dehumanizes.

Our purposes here are, first, to explain how Christianity relates to the historical and present-day forces which oppress Blacks and, second, to show how Blacks have rejected such a Christianity. We will then move on to indicate to Blacks the nature of true Christianity and a proper response to this Truth. Finally, we will suggest to White Christians some positive ways to make Christianity a force that meets the objective and subjective needs of the Black community.

True Christianity or a Sham?
Readers should understand that we use the term "Christi-

anity" (in quotes) as it is used by oppressed Blacks who have come to view it (apart from its denominational differences) as a monolithic whole. As we will show, the enslavement of Blacks was justified in the name of "Christianity." Blacks were made to feel cursed in the name of "Christianity." Blacks were excluded from White churches in the name of "Christianity." Blacks were (and are) excluded from the benefits of American life in the name of a "Christianity" which blesses the status quo.

Hence, we would like to make it clear that from this point on when we use "Christianity" we are using it in this broad, popular sense. Because we distinguish between White-racist "Christianity" and true Christianity (without quotation marks), the reader should be aware of the widest possible difference between these two (see chapter six). It is precisely this distinction that makes it incumbent upon Blacks to look again at Christianity. They should come to recognize that genuine Christianity affirms a positive Black self-image and actively cooperates with Blacks as they struggle to liberate themselves from White oppression.

1
Christianity and Slavery: 1619-1863

To develop an appreciation for present-day Black attitudes and roles with respect to organized Christianity, we must gain a historical perspective on slavery in the Western world. Obviously, slavery had economic and social dimensions. However, we will primarily consider the psychological impact not only on the slaves but on their posterity. A large part of racial conflict in America is grounded in this psychological dimension.

Slavery was an international phenomenon which developed in the United States as one aspect of the expansion of Western European culture into the New World. At one time or another almost every major European power promoted slave trade to North and South America. The Atlantic slave trade was "officially declared open" in 1441 when "ten Africans from the northern Guinea Coast were shipped to Portugal as a gift to Prince Henry the Navigator."[1] Following the discovery of the New World and for the next three and a half centuries, "and at an ever increasing momentum, the development of the new territories across the Atlantic demanded millions upon millions of African slaves."[2]

While it is difficult to determine how many Africans were captured for the slave trade, estimates range from ten to twenty million.[3] However, "it is more difficult to measure the effect of such an activity on African life" when it is remembered that "traders would have none but the best available slaves" and "that the vast majority of the slaving was carried on in the area of West Africa," the most highly civilized section of the continent with the possible exceptions of Egypt and Ethiopia.[4] Not only was African civilization dealt a severely debilitating blow, but the African slaves themselves who were captured, bought and transported to the New World suffered grossly inhumane treatment at the hands of White captors.

The process of slave "dehumanization" from moment of capture to moment of purchase parallels the concentration camp experiences of World War 2. The series of traumatic shocks had such an effect upon the Africans that their personalities were altered to suit the image and likeness of a system that assumed their inferiority.

First, there was the shock of being captured. "The second shock—the long march to the sea—drew out the nightmare for many weeks. . . . Hardship, thirst, brutalities, and near starvation penetrated the experience of each exhausted man and woman who reached the coast."[5] It was also shocking to be sold to foreign traders and then branded and herded into a strange ship. Then came the protracted and stupefying Middle Passage from Africa to the Americas. This dreaded transportation involved severe overcrowding, frequent rape, fatal disease and cruel beatings, all of which served to establish a master's absolute domination.[6] The final shock came with a seasoning period in the West Indies during which slaves were taught obedience and cringing submission to their masters.[7]

Black people were first forcibly introduced to the American mainland in 1619 when "Twenty Negars"[8] were sold as indentured servants by a Dutch trader to some inhabitants of Jamestown, Virginia. In this struggling colony, as in the others, there was not a pre-established system of slavery into which the Black man could fit. Rather, the slave system and its rationale were forged by Whites from latent racist tendencies and from the exigencies of life in the New World. Since White indentured servants or Indian slaves could not provide the permanent labor force for the development of the colonies, Blacks solved the problems.

As Africans came to America, they were easily "fitted" for work because they were divorced from their native culture and language. Their number was inexhaustible, and their physical characteristics made identification unmistakable. As rationale and justification for the system, they were (falsely) reputed to come from an uncivilized world, thus making slavery the means to the graces of White, Western, "Christian" civilization. W. E. B. DuBois states:

> A system at first conscious and then unconscious of lying about history and distorting it to the disadvantage of the Negroids became so widespread that the history of Africa ceased to be taught. . . . Without the winking of an eye, printing, gunpowder, the smelting of iron, the beginnings of social organization, not to mention political life and democracy, were attributed exclusively to the white race and to Nordic Europe.[9]

Thus, "by the end of the seventeenth century in all the colonies of the English empire, there was *chattel racial slavery* of a kind which would seem familiar to men living in the nineteenth century."[10]

The Masters' Tool

Christianity was a major barrier to be hurdled on the way to chattel racial slavery. There was an unwritten law that a Christian could not be held as a slave.[11] Therefore, if Blacks were allowed to be converted, they could no longer be slaves, and baptism would be tantamount to emancipation. This question was not settled in English law until 1729 when "the Attorney-General and Solicitor-General gave their formal opinions that baptism could not alter the temporal condition of a slave within the British kingdoms."[12]

The colonies did not hesitate to settle the problem much earlier. "If there were any laws, originally enacted to make Christianity more appealing, which might be construed as prejudicial to slavery, this danger could easily be removed by legislative authority."[13] To settle any doubt, the leading colony of Virginia in "a series of laws between 1667 and 1671 laid down the rule that conversion alone did not lead to a release from servitude."[14] Finally, the Church of England accepted the position stated by Morgan Godwyn in 1680 that "Christianity" and slavery were *fully compatible*.[15] Godwyn further argued that Christian faith made slaves better workers and served as security against infidelity and rebellion. The same themes were repeated in the nineteenth century.

With the problem of the status of Christian slaves settled, efforts were made to spread Christianity among the Blacks. In 1701 the Society for the Propagation of the Gospel in Foreign Parts (S.P.G.) was organized as a missionary arm of the Anglican Church. Its missionaries who worked among the slaves were opposed by slave masters who were reluctant to allow time to their slaves for religious instruction.

Some difficulty resulted too from the differences of opinion as to what tenets of religion should be taught the Negro and how they should be presented. Should the Negro first be instructed in the rudiments of education and then taught the doctrines of the church or should the missionaries start with the Negro intellect as he [sic] found it on his arrival from Africa and undertake to inculcate doctrines which only the European mind could comprehend? There was, of course in the interest of those devoted to exploitation, a tendency to make the religious instruction of the Negro as nearly nominal as possible only to remove the stigma attached to those who neglected the religious instruction of their servants.[16]

The Anglican effort had little impact on the slave community. Normally only those slaves closest to the master's family ("house niggers") became converts to Christianity while the greater number of field hands ("field niggers") were neglected.[17]

Those who were influenced were taught doctrine designed to support slavery, almost to the exclusion of the historic dogmas of the Christian faith. So, very early in colonial life an intimate and inseparable union between "Christianity" and the institution of slavery was effected. Other religious communions did not engage in significant evangelism or instruction among Blacks until the mideighteenth century. In fact, so ineffective was the work that an observer at the close of the American Revolution wrote: "One thing is very certain, that Negroes of that country, a few only excepted, are to this day as great strangers to Christianity . . . as they were at their first arrival from Africa."[18]

Not only were American "Christians" slow and ineffective in presenting the gospel to their Black slaves, but as indicated above they were also guilty of deliberately using the Christian faith to foster docility and obedience.

Through religious instruction the bondsmen learned that slavery had *divine sanction,* that insolence was as much an offense against God as against the temporal master. They received the Biblical command that servants should obey their masters, and they heard of the punishments awaiting the disobedient slave in the hereafter. They heard, too, that eternal salvation would be their reward for faithful service. . . .[19]

Many slaveholders reported that this kind of religious instruction had favorable effects on their slaves: There was greater enthusiasm for obedience and less thievery and mischief.[20] At all times, however, the religious activity of the slaves was necessarily supervised by the overseer or the master. Frequently, Blacks attended the same churches as Whites to insure proper instruction.[21] Discipline in these White-controlled churches was another tool of teaching obedience to the masters. Any infraction of the masters' will was cause for discipline or exclusion from fellowship until genuine repentance was made.[22]

At no time in Black slave history did slaves willingly or completely submit to the control of their masters. Because of this fact, a definite and detailed system of subjugation was devised. It might be called

the way to produce the perfect slave: accustom him to rigid discipline, demand from him unconditional submission, impress upon him his innate inferiority, develop in him a paralyzing fear of white men, train him to adopt the master's code of good behavior, and instill in him a sense of complete dependence.[23]

The "perfect slave" was rarely produced. Instead a slave was constantly watched by the overseer, restricted to the cabin after work hours, unable to leave the estate without a pass and unable to sell anything without a permit.[24] Slave marriages, as all other aspects of slave life, were under the direct supervision of the masters and had no legal significance. Only the master's consent was necessary for a marriage or divorce to take place.

Marriage among slaves was a farce, but not because of their

low station or ignorance of the ways of a nation. It was so because there could be no marriage where the nation moved monolithically and institutionally to keep all slaves exposed to capricious punishment. . . . By law no slave husband could protect his wife from physical or sexual abuse at the hands of a white man. By law no slave mother could protect her child against physical or sexual abuse at the hands of a white man. These were the reasons why marriage among slaves was meaningless. There could be no functioning family. . . .

The institutional structures of the nation [made] it impossible for the family to serve its primary purpose—*the protection of its members.*[25]

It is essential to note that any subsequent intellectual or psychological response of Black people to the institution of slavery would by definition be a response to a "Christianity" which was inextricably united with the oppressive forces of White dominance. Early in the Black experience with "Christianity" the image developed that Christianity is synonymous with Whiteness which is synonymous with oppression.

"Christianity" clarified its image during slavery by using the Bible to defend slavery. J. Oliver Buswell III has divided into four groups the historic scriptural justifications for slavery alleged by proslavery clerics and lay people:

(a) general assertions that the institution was natural, "ordained of God," and of benefit to the enslaved; (b) examples of slavery described or alluded to in the Bible, chiefly in the Old Testament; (c) instructions regarding behavior of slaves and masters, chiefly in the New Testament; and (d) underlying the whole structure of the defense system . . . the supposed teachings regarding the Negro race, chiefly based upon elaborations on the story of Ham and the curse of Noah.[26]

Defenders of slavery used these four categories of arguments in various combinations throughout the entire period. As the pressure of criticism coming from various quarters mounted, the biblical defense was maintained with great vigor.[27]

Southern divines gave great diligence to finding biblical support for slavery. They argued that "what God sanctioned in the Old Testament and permitted in the New, cannot be sin."[28] To call slavery a sin against God was therefore to question the authority of God's Word and be guilty of "doctrinal heresy." Other defenders of slavery asserted that God's rule of self-preservation and his desire for the good of the slaves required slaveholders to maintain the institution. The patriarchal system of slavery was designed so that a master should be "a guardian and a father" for the slaves; "freedom would be their doom; and equally from both they call upon us, their providential guardians, to be protected."[29] Noah's curse upon his grandson Canaan to be "a slave of slaves" was applied to all Africans and was supported by fantastic exegesis and erroneous logic.[30]

The Protesting Minority

A Christian minority did make efforts to attack the institution of slavery. In 1688 at the Monthly Meeting near Philadelphia, the Quakers presented a group resolution against slavery. Though the Yearly Meeting did not adopt it, "the resolution expressed a position which would gradually attract more and more Quakers."[31] Antislavery tracts and treatises appeared, and an open drive against Quaker slaveholding began. "This crusade, led by Benjamin Lay, John Woolman, and Anthony Benezet, resulted in positive action by the Philadelphia Yearly Meeting in 1758 against both slavetrading and slaveholding by Quakers."[32] Through these efforts many southern Quakers left the South and migrated into the Northwest Territory to avoid collusion with the sin of slavery.[33] By 1800

American Quakers had virtually ceased to be slaveholders.[34] Methodists also have a record of antislavery action. In 1780 the Baltimore Conference required its traveling preachers to set free the slaves which some of them held. They also proclaimed that "slave-keeping is contrary to the laws of God, man and nature, and hurtful to society, contrary to the dictates of conscience and pure religion."[35]

Christian criticism of slavery diminished after the Revolutionary War, in part because the temper of the country stressed unity and peace. Yet when the Abolitionist Movement later flourished, Christian voices were within its ranks. If the Bible could be used for proslavery arguments, it could surely be employed for antislavery arguments. Theodore Dwight Weld, who was a convert of Charles G. Finney,[36] argued that the essential spirit of the Bible opposed all slavery. In his popular and widely distributed work he charged that

ENSLAVING MEN IS REDUCING THEM TO ARTICLES OF PROPERTY —making free agents, chattels—converting *persons* into *things*—sinking immortality into *merchandise.*

We repeat it, THE REDUCTION OF PERSONS TO THINGS! Not robbing a man of privileges, but of *himself;* not loading him with burdens, but making him a *beast of burden;* not restraining liberty, but his neighbour of a *cent,* yet commission him to rob his neighbour of himself? . . . Slaveholding is the highest possible violation of the eight[h] commandment.[37]

Albert Barnes was another leading antagonist of slavery who battled on biblical grounds against "the vicious institution."[38] He met the proslavery argument and adduced his own scriptural evidence to show its fallacious reasoning.

The controversy over slavery naturally had divisive effects on the Christian denominations. Resolutions against slavery which had been passed by the Methodists were both difficult to enforce and actively opposed. As the southern states one by one passed legislation prohibiting the emancipation of slaves, enforcement became impossible.[39] This situation also was true for Baptist groups. However, as the radical and aggressive Abolition Movement grew in the North and the West and as slavery became an economically and psychologically "necessary" institution in the South, the churches divided over the question of slavery.

It is clear that the institution of slavery served the purpose of concretizing racist attitudes of White domination. The collusion of "Christianity" with this dehumanizing, oppressive institution made it inevitable for Blacks who were the victims of that oppression to conclude that "Christianity" was a mere extension of White-racist attitudes and must, therefore, be rejected and destroyed.

2
Christianity and Segregation: 1863-1914

Following the Emancipation Proclamation and the northern victory in the Civil War there was hope that former slaves would be granted the same rights and privileges that were enjoyed by Whites. But there were many obstacles to full equality.

First, the doctrine of Black inferiority was held widely both in the North and the South. Whites found social equality for Blacks practically inconceivable and many believed that because of the Black person's (supposedly) innate inferiority he would forever remain in the lower ranks of society. Indeed "some of the abolitionists themselves were ambivalent on the question of Negro equality."[1]

Second, the resistance of the South was forceful and fast. Slavery had been destroyed but the "southern mind" found other ways to perpetuate many of its assumed benefits. Southerners knew if little or nothing were done to provide Blacks with the skills and capital necessary to function freely they would remain in subjugation. To maintain White dominance, the White response to Black freedom was manifested in a series of "Black Codes." Although the Black Codes legalized Black marriages, permitted Blacks to hold and dispose of property, to sue and be sued, their main purpose was to keep the Black "as long as possible exactly what he was: a propertiless rural laborer under strict controls, without political rights, and with inferior legal rights."[2]

Finally, the status of the former slaves prohibited their fulfilling the many privileges and responsibilities of free people. As we have seen earlier, the entire system of slavery was deliberately structured to produce a "plantation mentality," giving the slaves a sense of inadequacy, a negative self-concept and dependency on the White world. Therefore, many "free" Blacks were inescapably held in bondage to their previous dehumanizing experience. Becoming "free" could not make them educated, stable, independent and self-reliant.

Reconstruction

The period of Reconstruction has afforded the substance for much historical debate.[3] Its history has great moral overtones and involves the deepest emotions of southerners and northerners. In recent years the one-sided interpretation which portrayed the southern Whites as victims of a brutal, foolish vengeance has been challenged and properly corrected by many historians.

President Andrew Johnson attempted to implement his inadequate plans for Reconstruction during the early months of his administration. When Congress met in the winter of 1865 it refused to admit the (so-called) Johnsonian governments from the eleven states that formed the Confederacy.[4] These governments were chiefly composed of former Confederate leaders. They had passed the Black Codes during their brief existence. Thus, as Congress began to develop its Reconstruction plans, a great conflict ensued with the president and many of the White southerners. The radical Republicans who favored "political equality" and special help for Blacks had real success. Through their efforts the Fourteenth and the Fifteenth Amendments to the Constitution were approved, the Freedmen's Bureau was created and supported, and governments of the southern states temporarily gave the former slaves political equality. However, the Radicals lost one important battle: the program of land reform was defeated. Kenneth Stampp remarks that

it meant that their [total] program would have only the most limited economic content; that the negroes' civil and political rights would be in a *precarious state for many years to come;* and that the radical influence in southern politics would probably collapse as soon as federal troops were removed.[5]

In addition, the greatest failure of the radical Reconstruction was that some of its vital features were short-lived. The Freedmen's Bureau which provided emergency relief, schools and protection for former slaves was disbanded in 1869 after its work had scarcely begun.[6]

The White southerners who desired to perpetuate Black subordination were hardly inactive during this period. The well-known Ku Klux Klan was only one of many volunteer organizations which "expected to do by extra or illegal means what had not been allowed by law: to exercise absolute control over the Negro, drive him and his fellows from power and establish, 'White Supremacy!' "[7] Not only were Blacks terrorized and murdered, but the few Whites who sympathized with them or helped them were also attacked. Through these and other political efforts the Reconstruction period "came to a gradual end as restraints were relaxed and stringent legislation repealed."[8] Eventually, the full-blown

system of segregation was legalized and the disenfranchise-
ment of Blacks proved successful.[9] "The South's demand
that the whole problem be left to the disposition of the dominant Southern white people" was accepted.[10]

By the end of Reconstruction the inequities of Blacks vis-
à-vis Whites had persisted. Blacks had been reduced to economic and political powerlessness in a society about to enter
the fullness of an industrial age. White institutional racism
continued to subjugate and exploit Blacks. White racism
switched its primary manifestation from slavery to segregation.

The latter decades of the nineteenth century and the early
years of the twentieth were marked by great White violence
against Blacks. The law stood helpless and ineffective while
thousands of Black men and women were brutally murdered
and terrorized. Even the North experienced violent antiblack
riots: New York, 1900; Springfield, Ohio, 1904; Greensburg,
Indiana, 1906; Springfield, Illinois, 1908.[11] Blacks were
"equal" citizens but they did not receive equal protection
under the law.

The Influence of the Churches

What role did White "Christianity" play in segregation? During the Civil War the churches of both North and South vigor-
ously supported the war effort. People not only prayed for
victory (believing that God was on their side) but they also
actively worked for victory by encouraging enlistment and
offering medical and religious aid. Both the Union and Confederate armies encouraged chaplains in their work. "Literature, provisions and comforts" were provided through
churches for soldiers engaged in the terrible conflict.[12] In addition, the northern cause was supported by outstanding
church leaders who, at their government's request, traveled
abroad to explain and justify federal policies. However, de-

spite a great rise in charities and missionary funds contributed by church people, "the cause of vital religion and morals undoubtedly suffered as a result of the war."[13]

The continued political and social involvement of Christian churches can be better understood with this background in mind. "The great northern churches, which had given an almost unanimous support to the government during the stress of the war, felt that they . . . had a . . . duty to take a hand in the solution of reconstruction problems."[14] On the other hand, the churches of the South came to be more concerned with defensive activity to support "the Southern way of life."

The independent regional course of development that the South was permitted to pursue following the Civil War fostered a growing sectional self-consciousness that was to manifest itself in the religious as well as in the political and intellectual life of the southern states.[15]

The three major denominations, Baptist, Methodist and Presbyterian, were unable to reunite after the war because bitterness from the separation and growing sectional interest overruled. The White southern churches developed a religious style and temperament that was nostalgic and defensive, serving only to widen the gap between themselves and northern churches.[16]

More central than the schisms was the fact that the White southern churches continued Black subservience in the name of God.

The [white] Protestant church, a major southern social institution, was among the first groups to segregate after the Civil War and to accept racism as the basis of race relations. Protestantism *helped pave the way* for the capitulation to racism at the turn of the century.[17]

If Blacks felt that they could turn to the "Christian" church for aid and comfort against the forces of racist attitudes and behavior, they were quickly disillusioned. The image of the irrevocable hostility toward Blacks by the White "Christian" church was perpetuated. Black people found no solace in the White church.

Though some effort at helping the freed slaves was made by White southern churches, hostile sentiment "in the South soon put an end to almost all official activity."[18] Many Black men and women "were anxious to separate themselves from the churches of their former masters" in order to express their freedom and to develop independently from White racist domination.[19] As a result, the Black church in the South grew rapidly.

Baptist and Methodist churches were by far the most popular among former slaves. The independent African Methodist Episcopal Church and the African Methodist Episcopal Zion Church which had been organized by freedmen in the North during the slavery period experienced phenomenal growth.[20] They were formed largely because White society would not tolerate the presence of Blacks as equals in common public worship. Thus the Black churches provided the first institution (and probably the only viable institution) which the freed slaves could develop independent from direct White control within the church itself.[21]

The Black church, from the period of the Civil War until World War 1, has been described as "the accommodative church."[22] The preachers in these churches oriented their members to White domination in society. As Black ministers had played the role of mediator and spokesman before the Civil War, so they continued during this period. In terms of race relations, the Black churches' main function was to accommodate their members to their subordinate status in White society.

The freedom of the Negro preacher was circumscribed by the fact that members of his congregation were in debt to whites or dependent upon whites for their jobs, and the very land on which the church stood was often the property of whites. The preacher was usually easily controlled, but if other means failed, he could be threatened with violence.[23]

The Black church not only maintained its function of accommodation by direct admonition but also indirectly by its *otherworldly orientation.*

In providing a structured social life in which the Negro could give expression to his deepest feeling and at the same time achieve status and find meaningful existence, the Negro church provided a refuge in a hostile white world. For [those] who worked and suffered in an alien world, religion offered a means of catharsis for their pent-up emotions and frustrations.[24]

Black minds were turned from the oppression and exploitation of this present world to a future world beyond the grave in which the faithful would be recompensed for all suffering and injustice. And Whites were glad to allow their Black folk a means of release which helped to keep them submissive. However, within this "happy" arrangement the Black preacher could often win minor concessions and favors from the White community, so long as his requests did not exceed whatever limits the Whites had established. Within this context it is clear that the church provided the only leadership for the Black community during the period.

The brief day of radical Reconstruction saw Black ministers serve in a great variety of governmental positions.[25] The Black church also provided social benefits to its community through its mutual aid societies and its efforts to stabilize the family.[26] At best the Black church was a mere extension of White-racist ideology wrapped in Black skins. Eventually many Blacks would come to view the Black church as a perpetuator of White control.

The positive significance of the Black church is that it gave many Blacks a survival style in a hostile world. Its weakness lay in its inability to define afresh the relationship of Black people to God and to their world. Instead, all too often, the Black church reinforced a plantation mentality that established "Whiteness" as the standard of fellowship with God and laid the basis for Black exclusion in worldly matters.

In contrast to White southern churches, White northern churches did provide some help to freed Blacks. In particular, this took the form of educational training. Since it had been illegal in much of the South to teach a slave to read, the greatest need was for literacy instruction.[27] During the years immediately following the war, hundreds of northern teachers, both men and women, went to the South to educate the former slaves. The work was difficult; harassment was common, and decent housing was hard to obtain. "The opposition to the missionary-teacher was based on a determination to keep the Negro 'in his place.' "[28] The total value of this movement was negligible even though many schools were established which later became leading Black universities. These efforts dissipated as radical Reconstruction failed.[29]

The zeal the White northern churches showed for the cause of Black people following the Civil War also waned during the late 1800s with the advent of secular and social forces that affected northern Protestants. Social Darwinism, racism and overseas expansion, including foreign missionary work, were among these influences.[30] In addition, desire for national unity and social problems centering in the cities diverted the northern churches from any strong protest against racial injustice. In fact, "they came close to accepting the South's 'solution' to the race problem."[31]

Racial segregation was expanded in the church and in the schools. Education for Blacks began to emphasize industrial and manual skills, thus insensibly fitting Blacks for a continued subordinate role in society. Protest against inequalities gave way to unflattering stereotypes of Blacks and to paternalistic attitudes. Even leaders within the social gospel movement neglected the racial problem and either adopted notions of racial superiority or refused to rebuke those who did.[32] Yet

if the proponents of the social gospel neglected the race problem, so did the great revivalists of the late nineteenth and early twentieth centuries. Before the Civil War the evangelic tradition was closely associated with the antislavery movement and social reform. The later revivalists tended to shy away from reform movements and to identify themselves with social conservatism. . . . In the North, Dwight L. Moody, the famed Chicago evangelist, *did not protest* against the white man's treatment of the American Negro. When Moody held revival meetings in the South, he did so on a segregated basis. . . . Years later, when Billy Sunday went South, he followed Moody's footsteps and held segregated meetings.[33]

Any society which deliberately singles out a group of people for a particular type of negative treatment based on an unchangeable factor (e.g., skin color) is, in effect, telling those people that they are not fit to participate in the benefits which naturally accrue to those living in that society. The overwhelming majority of Blacks in America during the segregation period were made to feel a profound and inescapable sense of personal inadequacy and political and economic impotence. The tragedy of the Black experience during segregation was that Blacks perceived "Christianity" as the chief support for the forces of racism that shaped these negative intrapsychic attitudes and social deprivations.

3

Christianity and Ghettoization: 1914-Present

Tracing the development of Black attitudes toward "Christianity" we observe, beginning with the twentieth century, one of the most significant phenomena in American history: the mass migration of Blacks to the cities of the North and West. Lerone Bennett signalized the importance of this influx by claiming that it nationalized the race problem, gave Blacks a base of potential political power in the North and set the stage for confrontation.[1] We refer to this period from approximately 1914 to the present as the ghettoization period in Black American history.

With the advent of this Black migration, a new and more subtle form of institutional racism developed. Black people were deliberately restricted to certain geographic areas and economic roles within the major cities and similarly reduced to political and economic chattel. The White Christian church was primarily acquiescent and complacent in the face of this Black subjugation.

The reasons for this migration involved both a "push" and a "pull." The push was the agricultural depression of the South. Increased production of quality cotton in the Southwest, increasing mechanization, the ravages of the boll weevil and a series of summer floods in 1915 were primary factors.[2] Another push was the continued terrorism against Blacks in the early decades of the twentieth century.

On the other hand, there was the great pull of the job opportunities in the industrialized North. Jobs in southern cities were filled first by Whites, leaving little or no work for Blacks.[3] So there was a natural and inevitable move northward to fill the labor demand created by World War 1 and by a series of Immigration Exclusion Acts. Similarly, World War 2 and the postwar boom continued this general demand for Black workers in the North.

This geographical redistribution and urbanization had tremendous effects upon the posture, not only of the Blacks who migrated, but also of the Blacks who remained in the South. Custom was broken, and openness to change was expressed. "Many Negroes were never exposed to the idea that they could be equal to whites, and they accepted their inferior status as an unchangeable aspect of the nature of things."[4] Since in the North the open, external forms of discrimination when expressed were expressed more subtly, Blacks throughout the country began to sense that the southern status quo was not divinely inspired. Therefore "with the increase in the number of Negroes in cities and in regions where whites openly espoused the ideal of racial equality, it was inevitable that negro pressure for elimination of racial discrimination would increase."[5]

Pressure did indeed increase. Urbanization in concentrated ghettos provided the first opportunity for Blacks to develop a sense of community which was combined with close physical proximity. Today it is obvious that ghettoization can produce political power with widespread effects on local and national elections.

The Kerner Report offers an excellent summary highlighting the reaction of Whites to the urban influx of Blacks since 1914.[6] In 1917 in East St. Louis, Illinois, there was a major antiblack riot issuing from a White fear that Blacks were endangering White status. The police did little to hinder White attacks on Blacks. "Streetcars were stopped, and Negroes, without regard to age or sex, were pulled off and stoned, clubbed and kicked, and mob leaders calmly shot and killed Negroes who were lying in blood in the street."[7] Because the Ku Klux Klan was reorganized and flourishing, "violence took the form of lynchings and riots, and major riots by whites against Negroes took place in 1917 in Chester, Pennsylvania, and Philadelphia; in 1919 in Washington, D.C., Omaha, Charleston, Longview, Texas, Chicago, and Knoxville and in 1921 in Tulsa."[8]

Racial disorders, usually antiblack riots by Whites, continued sporadically during World War 2. Such a riot was the Detroit riot of 1943 which was the most destructive and bitter. (It should be noted that the Harlem riot of 1943 was Blacks rioting against Whites. It resulted in destruction of property, looting and the burning of stores.[9])

The Black man's role in the armed forces during the two World Wars is also indicative of White attitudes and policy.[10] During both wars Blacks were forced to serve in segregated units, and only after a long struggle were Blacks allowed to train as officers for World War 1. Friction, antagonism and discrimination were prevalent phenomena both at home and overseas. However, both of the wars had a positive effect on the needs of Black Americans: They raised questions of the validity of America's democracy and justice for all citizens and they gave Blacks experience in other countries, thereby increasing the desire for change.

The changes that occurred during ghettoization encouraged the protest movement that formed during the early years of this century. Though Black people have continually protested their enslavement and subjugation,[11] it was only when the conditions of relative freedom prevailed that mass organizations began to grow.

The National Association for the Advancement of Colored People (NAACP) and the Urban League were the first protest organizations. They were distinctly interracial, believing that the rights of Black Americans would be won *within* the American democratic system. In the main, they protested legal blocks to political and economic participation by Black Americans. The Congress of Racial Equality (CORE) was formed in 1942 and the Southern Christian Leadership Conference (SCLC), which the late Dr. Martin Luther King, Jr., headed, was begun in 1957.[12]

Urban Racism

We have been at pains to emphasize that racist attitudes manifest themselves in institutional structures or forms. So it was that the newly migrated Blacks felt the impact of a new form of racism: urban racism. In trying to understand this period of continuing White domination, it must be understood that it is not easy to isolate overt racist action.

Maintenance of the basic racial controls is now less dependent upon specific discriminatory decisions and acts. Such behavior has become so well institutionalized that the individual generally does not have to exercise a choice to operate in a racist manner. The rules and procedures of the large organizations have already prestructured the choice. The individual only has to conform to the operating norms of the organization, and the institution will do the discriminating for him.[13]

Urban racism cannot *always* be attributed to some legal statute or explicit policy statement or ideology concerning the worth of Black Americans. Instead, urban racism represents in a term the synthesis of all White normative values and attitudes toward Black values and attitudes. These values and attitudes are concretized in the major economic, political and social institutions that perpetuate a set of differences between Blacks and Whites while maintaining a system of White domination.

This helps to explain why Blacks are more often unemployed than Whites, why Blacks must pay higher prices for goods and services than Whites, why Blacks live in poorer housing than Whites, why Blacks lack quality education, are relatively powerless politically and find it extremely difficult to break out from poverty and despair. Harold Baron describes the vicious cycle of poverty among Blacks:

The ghetto provides the base for the segregated schools. The inferior education in ghetto schools handicaps the Negro worker in the labor market. Employment discrimination causes low wages and frequent unemployment. Low incomes limit the market choices of Negro families in housing. Lack of education, low level occupations, and exclusion from ownership or control of large enterprises inhibit the development of political power. The lack of political power prevents black people from changing basic housing, planning and educational programs. Each sector strengthens the racial subordination in the rest of the urban institutions.[14]

The movement of the Black population from a rural to a predominantly urban setting had a tremendous impact both positively and negatively upon the structure of White "Christianity." The role of "Christianity" during this period did not assume the traditional forms of blatant racist expression. White "Christian" racism took on a more subtle and "acceptable" role and responded in a way that no longer involved it in direct segregation, discrimination and exploitation. "Christianity" during ghettoization had only to submit quietly to the prevailing racist attitudes and practices which had now become an *inseparable part* of urban institutions. It no longer had to provide explicit theological justification for White dominance in economic and political affairs or for segregation of Blacks from Whites in housing, education and social institutions. Because White "Christians" had participated in and had supported Black subordination throughout American history, it was no longer necessary for the White church to openly espouse White domination. In reality, the institutions themselves produced a set of differences between Whites and Blacks which guaranteed this domination.

Therefore, the sins of "Christianity" during ghettoization are no longer chiefly the sins of *commission* but of *omission*. This conclusion is not meant to deny the positive reaction of some Christians to the injustices perpetrated against Blacks by the larger White society. It is only intended to show that "Christianity" *as an institution* was, by and large, identified and implicated with the forces of urban racism.

After World War 1 some White denominations began to take "positive" interest in "the race problem." During the twenties the Ku Klux Klan revived, and racism was evident throughout the country as lynchings and rioting became common. Partly in response to these events, the Commission on Interracial Cooperation was formed and acted "to provide a better social climate for American Negroes, especially in the South."[15]

This interracial movement of the twenties and thirties was, however, often paternalistic and narrow in its goals.

The importance of the interracial movement should not be exaggerated. In certain respects it reversed the decline of interest in the race problem so noticeable in the decades preceding World War 1. . . . It did prod the churches to

look at the race problem. . . . But the basic approach of
Protestantism to a solution to the race problem still consisted of evangelism and Negro education.[16]
Such a superficial attack by White Christians on the symp-
toms of White racism did not begin to eliminate the causes of
racist exploitation. Clearly, while evangelism and education
were good moral efforts and served to soothe the conscience
of many White Christians, they did not begin to deal with the
harsh realities of institutional racism. This was, after all, the
cause of the social maladies and injustices.

In addition to the interracial movement, many major denominations during the thirties and forties passed resolutions condemning lynchings and brutality and calling for
equal opportunity. But as Frank Loescher wrote in the late
forties, "There is little evidence yet that the convictions of
the rank-and-file membership of Protestant denominations
are greatly influenced by these official actions."[17] In 1968
Kenneth B. Clark, a leading Black social psychologist, expressed the same sentiment:

> It's easy to see. Our churches make words; they pass reso-
> lutions. But there is no evidence that the churches have
> found the strength, the courage or the practical know-how
> to use religious institutions as instruments for bringing
> about the kind of maturity [that is necessary for justice in
> race relations].[18]

Great White Exodus

A concrete manifestation of White Christian inability and
unwillingness to cope with Black people and their needs is
expressed in their flight from the Black migration into the
cities. Gibson Winter described this White exodus in his
work, The Suburban Captivity of the Churches:

> Negro in-migration [which] increased rapidly during
> World War 1 and after 1920 . . . uniformly accelerated the

withdrawal of white Protestantism. . . . The retreat from
the Negro occurred in a two-phase movement: higher-
status congregations withdrew with the first threat of Negro invasion; middle- and lower middle-class congregations moved more slowly; consequently, the secondary
withdrawal of Protestantism came about through attri-
tion.[19]

The justifications usually given for this flight from Blacks
camouflage the real reason for the flight: the fear of Black
men having sexual relations with White women. This fear
has been traced back to the slavery period when Blacks were
totally dependent on Whites. Because of this, Whites began
to look on Blacks as objects of utility. Blacks, stripped of their
human dignity, were reduced to animal existence. Here we
find a gradual perversion taking place in the White man's
sexual outlook. He began to view White women as extraor-
dinarily pure and chaste. Simultaneously, he began to use
Black women for unrestricted sexual relationships. The Black
women could not resist the advances because of the power
the White men wielded in society.

White men respected the right of other White men to protect their families from sexual advances. Realizing that Black
men would have the same protective responses toward their
women, White men began to imagine that Black men were
obsessed with the desire to retaliate. The White man trans-
lated this obsession into a Black male's desire for sexual relationships with his own most precious possession—his pure,
White woman.

This could not help but lead to the fantastic exaggeration
in the white man's mind of the Negro male's sexual prowess. And this, in turn, would necessitate more repressive
measures against the Negro male—all caused by the white
man's guilt and anxiety. The necessity to "protect" the
white female against this fancied prowess of the male Ne-

gro thus became a fixed constellation in the ethos of the South.[20]

These sexual fears and mythologies today are not the sole expression of southern Whites, but indeed extend throughout all of the strata of White society—North and South. The sexual basis for White racism in America cannot be neglected: "In the core of the heart of the American race problem the sex factor is rooted; rooted so deeply that it is not always recognized when it shows at the surface."[21]

Physical proximity with Blacks, in the thinking of many Whites, produces the condition in which Black men can act out this supposed obsession. An illustration of this from personal experience involves a White community's response to enforced school desegregation in a southern town. A news reporter related to one of the authors that White mothers were seeking birth-control information to prevent having children, for such children would have contact with Blacks that might lead to interracial sexual relations. Though this is an extreme example, the fact is that such attitudes still exist. And they do more to prevent Whites from having permanent involvement on an equal basis with Blacks than any other set of racist attitudes.

We believe that, because of racist ideology and myths created by the White community in order to justify sexual exploits both in and out of slavery, there are some Black men and women who do desire sexual relations with Whites and vice versa. But a casual observation of the physical characteristics of so-called Black people in America indicates that White men should be held more in suspicion concerning sexual activity with Black women than Black men with White women.[22]

Eldridge Cleaver describes this sexual barrier to racial equality by constructing the fictional speech of a White male to a Black male:

I [the White male] will have access to the white woman and
I will have access to the black woman. The black woman
will have access to you—but she will also have access to
me. I forbid you access to the white woman. The white
woman will have access to me, the Omnipotent Adminis-
trator, but I deny her access to you, the Supermasculine
Menial. By subjecting your manhood to the control of my
will, I shall control.[23]

Thus Whites fled the cities as Blacks moved in, partly because
of this myth of the super Black male. This "Great White Exodus" reinforced the feelings of many Blacks that White
"Christianity" was insensitive and irrelevant to the Black
struggle. The exodus also perpetuated a negative self-concept among many Blacks who had embraced Christianity as a
means of finding self-esteem, acceptance and adequacy. But
above all, this White reaction to the Black migration clearly
told (and tells) Blacks that the "Christian" God was a White
God and that he was unwilling and incapable of accepting
Blacks as equals, unless they first whitened their skins and
their souls.

Another recent indication of White "Christian" rejection of
Blacks and Black concerns is the selection of "moral" issues
in America which are not high on the Black agenda. Groups
such as the Moral Majority seek to make America "moral"
by prohibiting abortions, gay rights and so on. But they say
little or nothing about the pregnant issue of White racism
which has oppressed and continues to oppress millions of
Blacks and people of color within America and throughout
the world.

Such picking and choosing of moral issues by Whites de-
nies the fundamental right of Blacks and others to be fully
human both before God and in society.

The Black church, which had given Black people a survival style in a hostile White world, responded to urbanization

and White withdrawal by developing a new mental outlook concerning its role in American society. The increasing economic diversity of the Black community in the city transformed the accommodative Black church into a secular church. As large middle-class and mixed-class congregations grew up in the urban center, the preacher was expected to devote more time to community affairs and the advancement of the race.[24] These activities, as always, were within the accepted limitations of the White power structure. They therefore consisted largely of improvements in housing, education and the like rather than in "social equality and integration with whites."[25]

Even within this change of perspective by Black churches, traditional loyalty to the Baptist and Methodist churches prevailed. But the predominantly otherworldly outlook and concern for the purely "spiritual" was diminished.[26] A number of the northern Black ministers became influential in politics and in protest. The Reverend Adam Clayton Powell, Jr., pastor of the huge Abyssinian Baptist Church in New York City, is a prime contemporary example of this. In his book, *Marching Blacks*, he calls for a religion with "ethical integrity" and "moral dynamic" which will transform the "churchianity" of modern-day religion.[27] Thus, there had crystallized among the mass of Black church people a new concept of the role of Christianity in everyday life situations and of the potential of Blacks to function in a more effective way in attacking the social injustices and inequities caused by White institutional racism.

Yet it was to be left to Blacks who repudiated "Christianity" as White (and therefore, inhuman and oppressive by its very nature) to create the atmosphere for Black people to redefine their whole lives independent of White "Christian" values. Because "Christianity" in the thinking of these awakened Blacks had become synonymous with the forces that

48   **What Color Is Your God?**

deprived Black people of a positive self-concept and of equal
political, economic and social participation in our society,
any future effort to "Christianize" Blacks would be met with
the response *"Your God is too white!"*

Our purpose is not to justify this response but to acknowledge the legitimate reasons Black people have for rejecting
Christianity based upon White "Christianity's" perennially
racist posture. It is an indisputable fact that White people did
use their version of Christianity to defend the "peculiar institution" and pacify their slaves. White people did relegate
their Black Christian brothers and sisters to separate pews
and galleries and, finally, separate churches. White people
have oppressed Black men and women in the name of the
God of the Bible throughout the entire history of America.

Pierre Berton, in *The Comfortable Pew,* issues this charge:

Indeed, the history of the race struggle in the United States
has been to a considerable extent the history of the Protestant rapport with the status quo. From the beginning, it
was the church that put its blessing on slavery and sanctioned a caste system that continues to this day. This has
prepared the way for the system of class structure within
the Protestant church that exists throughout the Western
world. It is a negation of that Christian equality before God
which the church preaches.[28]

This hypocrisy, Berton maintains, is what has driven thousands of people away from the organized Protestant relig-
ions. Moreover, those who are "most violently opposed to
white supremacy" are also fierce opponents of "Christian"
faith,[29] because "the church has been tried on the most fundamental Christian issue and found wanting."[30]

James Baldwin expressed similar attitudes in an interview
when he said that Black "people are repudiating the Christian church in toto." His White interviewer probed, "Are
they repudiating Christianity as well?" Baldwin shot back,

"No more intensely than you have." When further pressed about whether the Black church was dead in the North, Baldwin replied, "Let me rephrase it. It does not attract the young. Once that has happened to any organization, its social usefulness is at least debatable."[31]

Thus at present, there is a widespread disillusionment with "Christianity" among Blacks. Black people know they must redefine their identity in order to survive with dignity in a racist society, and to this end "Christianity" has proved a menace.

4
Glimpses of the New Identity

The historical review of the first three chapters has shown us the experience of Black Americans with institutions that sought to destroy or negate any sensitivity of Black people to their humanity and culture. During slavery the condition of Black people was so structured that a stereotypic personality that was consistent with racist ideology became pervasive. Black people were ripped from their native culture by a series of atrocities, deprived of a viable family unit, made to feel completely dependent upon White masters and deliberately exposed to White values and standards that reinforced their negative self-concept.

During the segregation period White Americans continued to deny Blacks full participation in the economic, political and social spheres of American life. Ghettoization brought with it a new form of institutional racism. A network of poor education, substandard housing and unemployment, a paucity of community services and political impotency deprived

Blacks of the full benefits of American life.

In the previous chapters the role of "Christianity" has been firmly established in relation to these oppressive institutional forces. Because of the inseparable nature of this relationship, many Blacks have come to feel that Christianity is synonymous with White exploitation, dehumanization of Blacks and the general perpetuation of White domination and Black subordination. "Christianity" is viewed by these Blacks as the last major obstacle to their attempt to recapture a sensitivity to their humanity and culture and to redefine their role in a White-racist society.

The necessity for Black Americans to redefine themselves should be evident to all. Any people who have been deprived of an understanding of their past and of a positive "people-concept" cannot hope to function as an equal and potent power in society. Black people in America have been deliberately deprived by White institutional forces of a sense of self-worth, thus reducing many to a state of psychological disarray and de facto powerlessness.

A positive or negative people-concept with the resulting self-concept is not the product just of group or internal psychological phenomena. Voices and images from the external world ultimately affect how the group and the individual view themselves. The White, American, "Christian" society in the periods of slavery, segregation and ghettoization communicated the idea that things associated with Black culture were evil, vulgar, diseased and primitive and that things associated with White culture were virtuous, beautiful, godlike and worthy of emulation. Racial dignity demands that Black Americans divest themselves of these aspersions cast upon them by Whites.

In tracing the present-day Black disillusionment with "Christianity," one must understand that throughout the history of this country there were many Blacks who rejected what appeared to be the White "Christian" concept of the worth and value of Black people. This chapter will consider the response of a few representative Blacks who rejected Whiteness as the standard of goodness and rejected "Christianity" as an oppressive tool in the hands of Whites who wanted to rob Blacks of their full humanity and citizenship.[1] This active pursuit and assertion of a positive Black identity laid the foundation for all Blacks who came after. Today's Black consciousness is the expression of these historical manifestations.

Beginnings
In the late 1700s Richard Allen and Absalom Jones shared a desire for Black participation and equality in those things which were considered "Christian." But being excluded from equal participation in Methodist church life, the two men departed from the traditional relations between Black people and White institutions, both secular and religious. The incident which precipitated this change took place in November of 1787 in Philadelphia.

Two prominent Negro leaders—Richard Allen and Absalom Jones—and several of their friends entered the St. George Methodist Episcopal Church for a regular Sunday service. Large numbers of Negroes had been drawn to this church and had been permitted to occupy comfortable seats on the main floor, but the increasing popularity of St. George's finally prompted church officials to announce that henceforth Negroes would be expected to sit in the gallery. Aware of this new seating arrangement, Allen, Jones, and other Negroes took seats in the front of the gallery, overlooking the places which they had previously occupied. But the church authorities had actually reserved an even less conspicuous place for their Negro worshipers in the rear of the gallery, and they soon made this quite

apparent. "We had not been long upon our knees," Allen
later recalled, "before I heard considerable scuffling and
low talking. I raised my head up and saw one of the trustees ... having hold of the Reverend Absalom Jones, pull-
ing him up off his knees, and saying, 'You must get up—
you must not kneel here.' " Jones thereupon requested that
the officials wait until the prayers had been completed.
When the trustees persisted, however, and threatened
forcible removal, "we all went out of the church in a body
and they were no more plagued with us." In fact, "we were
filled with fresh vigor to get a house to worship God in."[2]
This event led to the formation of two separate Black denominations. Absalom Jones organized the African Protestant
Episcopal Church of St. Thomas, and Richard Allen (in 1816)
became bishop of the African Methodist Episcopal Church
which he founded. Lerone Bennett, commenting upon the
importance of this separation of Blacks from White-racist
churches, states:

> By withdrawing from the white Methodist church, the
> little band of Negro Protestants affirmed the *new image*
> they had of themselves as human beings who demanded
> certain minimum concessions to their humanity.... The
> withdrawal raised large questions of identity.[3]
>
> They then embarked on a perilous journey of self-nam-
> ing, self-legitimization, and self-discovery.[4]

Christianity, as it was then expressed, was unwilling and
incapable of providing either equal participation for Blacks
or a set of values which would allow Black people to view
themselves positively. Therefore, this action of Richard
Allen and Absalom Jones in forming and controlling separate Black churches is an early glimpse of the use of positive
self-image and of power to build an independent base of true
Black expression in America. This too was a rejection by
Blacks of the "Christian" God who is too White and by virtue

of his Whiteness is incapable of empowering his followers to accept Blacks as equals.

Another significant departure in the thinking of Blacks toward their role in White society was revealed in Nat Turner's 1831 slave rebellion. Nat Turner was a self-taught Black slave who very early in his life rejected the notion that Blacks were inferior to Whites. Much of his thinking about his own equality and worth came from the Bible. Naturally, therefore, he rejected the White "Christian" teaching that Blacks were cursed by God and meant to serve Whites all their lives. Nat Turner considered himself a divine appointee to execute God's judgment against Whites. He states in his *Confessions*:

On the 12th of May 1828, I heard a loud noise in the heavens, and the Spirit instantly appeared to me and said the Serpent was loosened, and Christ had laid down the yoke he had borne for the sins of men, and that I should take it on and fight against the Serpent, for the time was approaching when the first should be last and the last should be first.[5]

Not only was Nat Turner motivated by what he felt was a divinely given mission to destroy Whites, but he also seemed to be obsessed with a desire to obtain his own freedom. In August of 1831, Nat Turner and a band of sixty to eighty Black compatriots roamed the countryside of South Hampton, Virginia, terrorizing, killing (forty-five Whites) and demonstrating Black resistance to slavery.

The significance of this rebellion for our purposes is that a representative number of Blacks rejected the traditional White "biblical" justification for Black inferiority. They felt that they could be used as instruments in the hand of God (who obviously accepted their equality and worth) to destroy Whites who carried out injustices against Blacks. W. E. B. DuBois interpreted Nat Turner's rebellion as a repudiation of the accepted notion that Black people are nobodies:

Why strive to be somebody? The odds are overwhelming
against you—wealth, tradition, learning and guns. Be rea-
sonable. Accept the dole of charity and the cant of missionaries and sink contentedly to your place as humble
servants and helpers of the white world.[6]

Another prominent Black protest leader, Frederick Douglass,
vented his indignation against the White "Christian" hypocrisy that forced Blacks to sit in an "African corner," a
"Nigger Pew," in seats marked, "B. M." for Black Members,
or in the balcony, "Nigger Heaven."

Attending a Methodist service in New Bedford, Frederick
Douglass found himself placed in a separate seat and saw
his brethren stand meekly aside as the whites attended the
Lord's Supper. The pastor then called upon his "colored
friends" to come forward, declaring, "You, too, have an interest in the blood of Christ. God is no respecter of persons."
By this time Douglass had had enough. "The colored members—poor, slavish souls—went forward as invited. I went
out, and have never been in that church since."[7]

Frederick Douglass further denounced the "Christian" attitude toward Black people in a speech in Rochester, New
York, on July 5, 1852. He expressed not only his own feelings, but the emotions of Black people of all ages.

But the Church of this country is not indifferent to the
wrongs of the slaves. It actually takes sides with the oppressors. It has made itself the bulwark of American slavery, and the shield of American slave-hunters. Many of its
most Eloquent Divines, who stand as the very lights of the
Church, have shamelessly given the sanction of religion
and the Bible to the whole slave system. They have taught
that man may properly be a slave; that the relation of master and slave is ordained of God; that to send back an es-
caped bondman to his master is clearly the duty of all the
followers of the Lord Jesus Christ; and this horrible blas-

phemy is palmed off upon the world for Christianity.

For my part, I would say, welcome infidelity! Welcome atheism! Welcome anything! In preference to the gospel, as preached by those Divines! They convert the name of religion into an engine of tyranny and barbarous cruelty. . . . These ministers make religion a cold and flinty-hearted thing, having neither principles of right action nor bowels of compassion. They strip the Love of God of its beauty and leave the throne of religion a huge, horrible, repulsive form. It is a religion for oppressors, tyrants, man stealers, thugs. . . . A religion that favors the rich against the poor: which exalts the proud above the humble; which divides mankind into two classes, tyrants and slaves; which says to the man in chains, *Stay there* and to the oppressor, *Oppress on!!*[8]

The Black church as a whole revealed its rejection of White "Christianity" in a unique manner: through what we have come to know as the Black spirituals. The protest elements of the spirituals are seen in the choice of themes about which the Black slaves sang. Because they rejected the White distortions of Christianity which stressed the divine approval of slavery, the slaves sang "about Joshua and the battle of Jericho, Moses leading the Israelites from bondage, Daniel in the lions' den. . . . Here the emphasis was on God's liberation of the weak from the oppression of the strong."[9]

This theme of liberation in the spirituals was firmly based upon the biblical view that "God's righteousness is revealed in his deliverance of the oppressed from the shackles of human bondage."[10]

W. E. B. DuBois was one of the seminal thinkers of the Black protest-identity movement. His opinions of Christianity and its role vis-à-vis the Black struggle in America against oppressive, dehumanizing forces were succinctly expressed in 1931.

The church, as a whole, insists on a divine mission and guidance and the indisputable possession of truth. Is there anything in the record of the church in America in regard to the Negro to prove this? There is not. If the treatment of the Negro by the Christian Church is called "divine," this is an attack on the conception of God more blasphemous than any which the church has always been so ready and eager to punish.[11]

According to DuBois, the validity of Christianity stands or falls with the Christian church's actions. It is understandable that such a man, greatly influenced by his vast historical research concerning the destructive role of Christianity in relation to Black people, would conclude that Christianity (as it was then expressed and structured) was totally incapable of helping Black people redefine and reorder their existence in American society.

The Renaissance

The White concept of God, goodness, beauty and truth was frequently expressed by Black writers during the period of ghettoization. With the Harlem Renaissance of Black expression in a great variety of literary forms, the theme of "God is White" was often manifested. Langston Hughes, in his popular Jesse B. Semple stories, wrote of the impressions that Semple had of the experience of heaven for a Black man. Semple, after being told that he must be born again and "washed whiter than snow" to erase his birthmark of Blackness, retorted by saying,

Imagine all my relatives setting up in heaven washed whiter than snow. I wonder would I know my grandpa were I to see him in paradise? Grandpa Semple crowned in Glory with white wings, white robe, *white skin* and golden slippers on his feet! Oh, Grandpa, when the chariot swings low to carry me up to the Golden Gate, Grandpa, as I enter

will you identify yourself—*just in case I do not know you,*
white and winged in your golden shoes? I might be sort of
turned around in heaven, Grandpa.[12]
Jesse B. Semple's representative Negro desire to become White
is revealed in his conversation with Saint Peter and a White
southern governor at the gate of heaven. The governor in-
sisted that Jesse enter heaven through the back COLORED
ENTRANCE. When Saint Peter could do nothing, Jesse said:
"I did not realize I was in hell. . . . I thought when I riz
through space from my dying bed, I had landed at the Gate
of Heaven. Anyway, Peter, is not my sins washed whiter
than snow? Am I not *white now inside and out?*

Whereupon, Old Down-home Governor spoke up and
said, "You have to bathe in the River of Life to be washed
whiter than snow. The River of Life is in heaven. You are
not inside yet, Semple. Therefore, you are still black.
White is right, black get back! You are not coming in the
front entrance."[13]
Although Jesse B. Semple is a fabricated character who moves
through the hostile world of Harlem, he nevertheless accurately reflects the experiences of many Blacks with White
"Christianity." In particular, James Baldwin, in relating his
own personal life in Harlem and the need for young Blacks to
get a "gimmick" in order to survive amid the oppressive and
destructive forces created by urban racism (such as sexual
perversity, drugs and racketeering), tells of his encounter
with the White God. Baldwin determined that his gimmick
for survival in Harlem would be the church. He relates that
while in church one summer night he fell victim to the strang-
est sensations of his life after hearing a woman preach. He
began clapping and singing, stomping and falling to the floor
trying to get a "salvation experience." At his highest moment of emotion and ecstasy he looked up from the floor, trying to get a sense of power and acceptance. He revealed his

innermost feelings and sense of frustration by saying: "But God—and I felt this even then, so long ago, on that tremendous floor, unwillingly—is *white.* . . . I found no answer on the floor—not *that* answer, anyway—and I was on the floor all night."[14]

James Baldwin was a Black man seeking an experience with God in a White man's world. He was driven away from God because of his acute awareness of "Christianity's" identification with oppressive and dehumanizing institutions. Baldwin represents the commonality of experience for many Blacks with White "Christianity." Like Jesse B. Semple, he is typical.

Malcolm

Every significant movement against human injustices and atrocities goes through a period of expression in which one man eloquently carries the grievances and agonies of the oppressed people. Malcolm X, in our opinion, represents that Black man who eloquently and lucidly stated the Black man's case against White "Christianity." He symbolizes a redefined Black man who has now found meaning, worth and value independent of White definitions and values.

Malcom X demanded of his Black brothers and sisters that they throw off every vestige of Whiteness in order to be free people and to find a new source of power consistent with their rediscovered humanity. To Malcolm, high on the list of negative forces and ideologies was "Christianity." It must be exposed as inextricably united with oppressive forces in a racist society. It must be rejected as a religion which seeks to rob Black people of their humanity and deprive them of the physical means whereby they can correct social injustices.

In his widely circulated *Autobiography* Malcolm pointedly states: "Christianity is the white man's religion. The Holy Bible in the white man's hands *and his interpretations of it* have been the greatest single ideological weapon for enslaving millions of non-white human beings."[15]

Malcolm builds his case for the Black rejection of Christianity by maintaining that Black people

> were supposed to be a part of the "Christian Church," yet we lived in a bitter world of dejection . . . being rejected by the white "Christian Church." In large numbers we became victims of drunkenness, drug addiction, reefer smoking . . . in a false and futile attempt to "escape" the reality and horror of the shameful condition that the Slavemaster's Christian religion had placed us in.[16]

Malcolm puts the final touches to his denunciation of White "Christianity" as a destructive force by citing its greatest failure: failure to eliminate racism within its own structures. He asks:

> And what is the greatest single reason for this Christian church failure? It is the failure to combat racism. It is the old "You sow, you reap" story. The Christian church sowed racism—blasphemously; now it reaps racism.[17]

It is of paramount importance to empathize with the experiences of these Black protesters and to understand their subsequent rejection of a hollow, hypocritical and racist "Christianity." Their experiences represent the inner-psychological responses of countless Black people to a White God who is associated with forces that seek to make Black people insensitive to their humanity and politically and economically powerless.

We live in a day in which many Black people still feel it imperative to redefine themselves independently of all White standards, values and definitions. An expression of this phenomenon has been Alex Haley's *Roots* which galvanized large and diverse segments of the Black community in a search for the Black American past both in Africa and in the United States. To be sure, many nonblacks were affected by *Roots* in that they were forced to alter their views about Blacks. But the Black appreciation of Haley's work demonstrates conclusively the need to move consciously and deliberately toward an independent Black self-understanding. This Black consciousness can be seen as a total rejection of White "Christianity" by many Blacks who seek a new identity of pride and power, both collective and personal.

5
The Emergence of Black Consciousness: The Basis for a New Religion

A survey of the Black protest against White "Christianity" reveals widespread Black disillusionment and rejection of the basic values, assumptions and attitudes of White, American "Christianity." "Christianity" as the national religion has become synonymous with the oppressive institutions of White racism which seek to perpetuate the social, economic and political subordination of Black Americans. It has, in effect, done its greatest damage in conditioning Black people to hate themselves and all things associated with Blackness. People who hate themselves are not psychologically equipped to function as equal and potent members of any society.

Black people sense today (and have always sensed) that black-skinned Americans must redefine themselves and their role *according to their own values*, assumptions and goals in order to survive in a White-racist society. The tragedy of the Black experience in relation to "Christianity" is

that "Christianity" (as manifested in its association with dehumanizing institutions) was and is unable to provide Blacks
with the necessary basis to free themselves from White oppression and a sense of inferiority. Thus, there has crystallized within the Black community a consciousness and sensitivity to Black humanity and to the Black past and future.
This new awareness and its social expression is called *Black
consciousness*. (Formerly the phrase *Black power* was used.)

Black consciousness in our opinion is both a *subjective*
and an *objective* force. It is subjective in that the Black individual's psychological constitution is refocused on his humanity and worth. It is objective in that Black people collec-
tively express an awareness of this redefined self when they
deal with institutions which subordinate them. We will deal
with each manifestation in turn.

Black Self-Image

The negative forces in operation during the periods of slavery, segregation and ghettoization have had the collective
effect of creating in the minds of many Black people doubts
concerning their human worth and dignity. The humanity
of Blacks in America was primarily left to be determined by
the opinions and attitudes of the dominant White society.
America's founding fathers assumed it was within their
power and responsibility to debate, compromise and nego-
tiate the human worth of Black people. Probably no other
single issue has created more conflict and division among
Whites. To this day, the power of White "Christian" society
to define the ultimate worth of Black people and Blackness
has created within many Blacks a doubt about their equality
with Whites. W. E. B. DuBois expressed the Black person's
uncertainty by posing the following queries:

To be sure behind the thought lurks the afterthought: sup-
pose if all the world is right and we are less than men? Sup-

pose this mad impulse is all wrong, some mock mirage from the untrue? . . . a shriek in the night for the freedom of men who themselves are not yet sure of their right to demand it?[1]

Black consciousness is the bold assertion of the fact that the humanity of Blacks is a non-negotiable, indisputable reality. The humanity of Black people *is!*

Black consciousness is *initially* the psychological realization that White oppressive, dehumanizing institutions are only capable of making Blacks insensitive to their humanity. No man or institution has the power to destroy the basic humanity of Black people. The reality of the humanity of Blacks is independent of racist attitudes and values. The humanity of Blacks is as certain as the forces used by God to regulate the universe, as real as the principles that dominate life and death.

People and the institutions that reflect their values are inhuman and oppressive when they deliberately single out another group of people for the purpose of subjugating and making them more concerned with survival in a hostile environment than with basic human issues. These basic human issues with which Blacks should be concerned are: Who am I? Where did I come from? Where am I going? What is to be my role and the role of others like me in the larger society?

Regardless of the extensive economic, political and educational control Whites have held over Blacks, the essential White power in America must ultimately be measured by White ability to control Black minds. For any group that can dictate the terms and definitions by which another group defines itself possesses real power. Black consciousness acknowledges that.

Thus any Black objection to the forces of destruction and exploitation *must* begin at the level of the mind. Black consciousness begins with the realization that many Blacks have been conditioned by White institutions to hate themselves and to question their basic worth. After a confrontation with these negative psychic forces, Black consciousness reaffirms the indestructibility of Black humanity and actively seeks values and definitions that will allow Blacks to reorder their lives in White America.

The normative values of our "Christian" culture make it impossible for Blacks to view themselves as equals with Whites. The very institutions that reflect White America's values are predicated on the assumption and ideal of the superiority of Whites and the inferiority of Blacks. These values have already been shown to exist in White "Christian" society's justification of the enslavement of Blacks and in its justification of their continued economic and political exclusion.

Black consciousness as a force drives the newly sensitized Black person back to Africa to find his existence and sense of history independent of the "Sambo" plantation-induced mentality. Blacks are made to see that the glory of the ancient kingdoms of Ghana, Mali, Songhay and so forth—the splendor and the power, the agonies and the joys, the contributions of Ethiopia and Egypt—are theirs. Africa *functions* to make Blacks see that they had a culture and a history *independent* of White-racist America. Though this humanity cannot in reality be defined by anyone, the questions that lurk in Black minds about their human worth and value have now been resolved: I am human—proud, indomitable, irrepressible!

An awareness of Black contributions to American life also gives "redefined Blacks" greater certainty of their human qualities and worth. They see, amid the negative and destructive forces created by White racism, that Black men and women such as Benjamin Banneker, Harriet Tubman, Denmark Vesey, Gabriel Prosser, Marcus Garvey, Sojourner Truth, A. Phillip Randolph and Charles Drew not only helped develop a survival style and culture uniquely Black, but also made contributions of lasting value to the larger American society.

Black consciousness is a repudiation of the notion that the Black experience in America is maladaptive, pathological and diseased. Rather, it is a demonstration of the desire and power of a people to survive and excel.[2]

This subjective concept of Black consciousness is not shared by all black-skinned Americans. It is vital that distinctions be made between types of black-skinned people on the basis of their demonstrated sensitivity (or insensitivity) to Black consciousness as a subjective force. We believe there are three broad characterizations of black-skinned people in America: Black, Negro and "street nigger."

A *Black* is an individual who has come home to Blackness, who has repudiated White concepts and values about her or his role and worth in America. This person defines himself using his own terms, definitions and values. The Black person believes that one must use whatever means necessary to deal with the oppressive forces created and perpetuated by White racism.

A *Negro* is a black-skinned person with a White mind. He or she has set as a goal the emulating and approximating of the White world; he wants to look White, think White and behave White. Because of his controlled participation in the pursuit of materialism, the Negro is made to believe that all is not as bad as stated by Blacks and other dissidents.

A *"street nigger"* is the personification of all those negative and distorted White concepts of the nature and worth of Blacks. He or she usually represents the epitome of the White concepts of Black sexual prowess, recklessness, proclivity toward crime and so on. He is the modern-day result of the negative conditioning of White institutional racism. He hates himself and other Blacks. The "street nigger" is insensitive to his humanity and daily falls victim to the direct exploitation and oppression of White society.

We realize that definitions and categories of the type which we have given cannot possibly describe all the responses of black-skinned people to oppression and discrimination.[3] But it is our belief that the above analysis reveals their basic, characteristic response to racist forces.

The failure to recognize these differences can have catastrophic results for those who are trying to understand and cope with the Black psychic revolution. Many, for example, may feel that by dealing with the Negro they are helping to solve the racial problem in America; they are not cognizant of the fact that the Negro's basic viewpoint on life makes him just as oppressive and threatening to Blacks as is the White world. Therefore, it is imperative that one sincerely concerned with being a part of the solution to the problems of racism recognize and have appropriate dealings with all three types of Black people.[4]

The concept of Black power as a subjective force among Blacks was summarized by Carmichael and Hamilton in the 1960s as:

the need [of Blacks] to assert their own definitions, to reclaim their history, their culture; to create their own sense of community and togetherness. There is a growing resentment of the word "Negro," for example, because this term is the invention of our oppressor; it is his image of us that he describes. Many blacks are now calling themselves African-Americans, Afro-Americans or black people because that is our image, stereotypes—that is, lies—that our oppressor has developed will begin in the white community and end there. The black community will have a positive image of itself that it has created. This means we will no longer call ourselves lazy, apathetic, dumb, good-timers, shiftless, etc. Those are words used by white America to define us. If we accept these adjectives, as some of us have in the past, then we see ourselves only in a negative way, precisely the way white America wants us to see ourselves. Our incentive is broken and our will to fight is surrendered. From now on we shall view ourselves as African-Americans and as black people who are in fact energetic, determined, intelligent, beautiful and peace-loving.[5]

Structural Change

As we have defined Black consciousness, the subjective (psychological) force must manifest itself in objective reality. The initial psychological forces as analyzed *are not enough in themselves to emancipate an oppressed people.*

A people are not simply free when they have unshackled their minds from the negative concepts and values of the oppressor; they are free when the combined forces of the mind .and the body unite with people of similar experience to deal with the institutions which keep them in economic and political slavery.

The Grand Inquisitor, in Dostoyevsky's great work *The Brothers Karamazov,* observed that the real ruler of humanity is "he who holds their conscience *and their bread* in his hands."[6] Black consciousness wisely recognizes that Black people will always be victimized and dominated by White society if Blacks do not control their economic and political destiny. Aimé Cesaire, in his speech at the Conference of Negro-African Writers and Artists in 1956 as reported by James Baldwin, expressed this truth:

All cultures have ... an economic, social, and political base, and *no culture can continue to live if its political destiny is not in its own hands.* "Any political and social regime which destroys the self-determination of a people also destroys the creative power of that people."[7]

Thus if the Black community is to manifest its values and ideals in ways which affirm and express its full humanity, it must deliberately structure its daily affairs and institutions. Black people must establish independent and viable bases of economic and political power. To many Americans such an independent expression of Black consciousness would seem to be synonymous with separatism and Black racism. However, in a pluralistic society like our own in which Blacks are victims of White domination, it is an absolute necessity for Black people to develop independent power bases if they are to assure themselves and their posterity of the legacy of the Black experience and of equal opportunities free of White-racist control.

No group of people can in reality be said to possess power as long as they continue to simply *react* to oppressive forces. The objective power of a people can be measured by their ability to initiate and control their own circumstances. This reality means that Black people must control the *educational systems* that teach their young. Only in this way can Black children learn to develop a positive self-concept and a desire for political, economic and social participation both within and without the Black community. They must see Black men and women in decision- and policy-making positions in their educational systems in order to encourage and reinforce a sense of adequacy and competence.

This reality means that Black people must control their *political representatives* so that the needs and desires of their community are consistently expressed and met at all levels of government. Any political coalitions will be to the mutual benefit of the Black community and all others involved. This reality means that Black people must support Black enterprises so as to establish an economic base among Blacks that will allow Black entrepreneurs to participate in the larger American economy in viable coalitions.

This understanding of Black consciousness in its objective expression in the educational, political and economic spheres is found in a classic statement by Carmichael and is found in Hamilton.

Black Power [Black consciousness] recognizes—it must recognize—the ethnic basis of American politics as well as the power-oriented nature of American politics. Black Power therefore calls for black people to consolidate behind their own, so that they can bargain from a position of strength. But while we endorse the *procedure* of group solidarity and identity for purpose of attaining certain goals in the body politic, this does not mean that black people should strive for the same kind of rewards (i.e., end results) obtained by the white society. The ultimate values and goals are not domination or exploitation of other groups, but rather an effective share in the total power of the society.[8]

Black consciousness in no way seeks to negate the humanity of Whites. Rather it confronts Whites with the reality that the values and traditions of power distribution in America have made Whites incapable of accepting Blacks as equals. Therefore, any change in White attitudes toward Blacks must be a direct result of Black assertiveness in all spheres of life. Whites can only be free of their racism as they are forced to view Blacks (using definitions of Blacks and being confronted by Blacks) as human, political and economic equals. Only when this becomes a reality will there be a demise of racism as manifested in White paternalism, ignorance and fear.

Black consciousness cannot guarantee to Whites totally nonviolent responses in the Black person's quest for political and economic equality. Black people will use any means necessary to achieve full equality in a society founded on the ideal of the "inalienable rights of men." Whites must realize that Black consciousness is not predicated on violence or

nonviolence but on the survival and full participation of
Blacks in the benefits of American society. It is this dedica-
tion to the right of Black people to survive that will determine
whether Black people will respond violently or nonviolent-
ly to racist forces. It is suicidal for Black people in light of
the legacy of violence committed against them by Whites to
accept nonviolent, purely legal tactics: "To expect... the
[Black] community to show neither anger nor hate, neither
fear nor violence, when their values are challenged and their
aspirations frustrated is to ask for the impossible."[9]

The Relevance to Religion

We are trying to understand the disillusionment and disen-
chantment of many Blacks with White "Christianity." In
this respect Black consciousness functions as an ideological
base of spiritual awareness for those Blacks who realize the
spiritual dimension of their humanity but who cannot identify and intimately associate with what they conceive to be
a White, blue-eyed Jesus—a Jesus who negates the humanity
of their Blackness, a Jesus who demands that they Whiten
their souls in order to be saved.

Black consciousness as a subjective and objective force
does not pretend to be able to meet the spiritual needs of
Blacks. But, as advocated and developed by individual
Blacks and Black organizations, it does contain a body of
impressions about what role religion ought to play in the
life of the "new Black."

Black consciousness indicates to Blacks that any experience with God, in light of their everyday exploitation and
persecution, is only real and beneficial if that God can actively empathize with them and act against those forces which
seek to destroy them. Black consciousness indicates that God
must be made over into an image and likeness consistent
with redefined Blackness: God must be able to deal with

Black children who are victimized daily by poor education, malnutrition, rats and roaches; a Black man who is unemployable; a Black woman whose infant son has died of lead poisoning from eating fallen paint chips in a dilapidated apartment; a young Black student who senses the shame and hypocrisy of the so-called democratic ideals of the White world.

In reality God must become Black. He must become the God not of the "sweet by and by" but of the bitter here and now.

Black consciousness provides the impetus which drives a Black person to dictate the terms of agreement with any religion. There has been developing within a substantial segment of the Black community a distinct body of theology— Black Theology. The major goal of Black Theology, which is often labeled as "liberation theology," is to redefine religion in terms which minimize its otherworldly and futuristic elements and maximize its concern for daily needs and for the attempts of Black people to assert their humanity and establish political and economic power. With this understanding, Black Theology is a continuing expression of a historical rejection of White Christianity on the part of many Black people. It is in part a fulfillment of the need that Richard Allen and Absalom Jones felt for a religion that would recognize the human equality of Blacks; in part a fulfillment of the need that Frederick Douglass felt for a religion that would identify with the needs of the oppressed poor; in part a fulfillment of the need that W. E. B. DuBois expressed for a religion that reflects a creed of love and brotherhood in practical, concrete actions; in part a fulfillment of the need that Langston Hughes's Jesse B. Semple had for a religion which allowed him to relate to God without negating his Blackness. In a very real sense, Black Theology asserts that God has become incarnate or immanent in such a way that he can relate to the needs of oppressed Black people.

As Julius Lester has said, God then becomes "the God of Nat Turner and Rap Brown, the God of Muddy Waters and B. B. King, the God of Aretha Franklin and the Impressions, this great God Almighty Everlasting *et in terra pax hominubus,* and all them other good things."[10]

One of the most significant expressions of early Black Theology outside the Christian tradition in the twentieth century was that of the Black Muslim movement under the leadership of the Honorable Elijah Muhammad.[11] Mr. Muhammad sensed in the late thirties the need of the Black masses to redefine their religious experience independent of White-racist "Christianity." He embraced and developed a theology which he believed to be consistent with the religion of Islam. The Black Muslims did not seek to restructure Christianity so that it provided a religious expression for Blacks, but totally repudiated Christianity as a tool of oppression and as an ideology that perpetuated Black exclusion.[12]

As indicated by Louis Lomax, the impact of this movement on the development of Black Theology and social protest was that the indictment of Christianity by the Black Muslims:

forced thoughtful Negro Preachers into an almost impossible position. . . . I have talked this over with scores of Negro clergymen, and almost to a man, they agree that Muhammad has deeply shaken the Negro Christian community. Muhammad's recital of how the Christian faith has failed the Negro—"By their fruits ye shall know them"— has sunk deeper into the hearts of the Negro masses than Negro clergymen will admit publicly.[13]

Moreover—and this is the important point—"no gospel that fails to answer Muhammad's criticism of Christianity will be accepted."[14]

Another popular expression of Black Theology in its early stages which attempted to answer Muhammad's criticisms by reformulating Christianity was developed by Albert Cleage of the Shrine of the Black Madonna in Detroit. He espoused a religious ideology which, in his thinking, restored Blackness and truth to the history of ancient Israel, Jesus and Christianity.[15] For Cleage, Blacks need not reject Christianity but only a White, "honkified" perversion of it. Because Christianity has been twisted and distorted by racists, many Blacks, according to his argument, have developed a White Jesus who sanctions and blesses the atrocities committed by Whites against Blacks. Cleage feels that it is crucial that the Black identity of Jesus be exposed.

When I say that Jesus was black, that Jesus was the black Messiah, I'm not saying, "Wouldn't it be nice if Jesus was black?" or "Let's pretend that Jesus was black." I'm saying that Jesus WAS black. There never was a white Jesus. Now if you're white you can accept him if you want to, and you can go through psychological gymnastics and pretend that he was white, but he was black. If you're such a white racist that you've got to believe he was white, then you're going to distort history to preserve his whiteness.[16]

Cleage reconstructed a Jesus whose whole life was spent in challenging and seeking to destroy forces of racism represented by White Roman power. He believed that Black people have a similar mission toward institutional racism by reordering and redefining their lives to gain an independent base of power.

Cleage's challenge to all Blacks who desire an experience with Christianity is that they must repudiate a White Christ. Until they do so,

they have not freed themselves from their spiritual bondage to the white man nor established in their minds their right to first class citizenship in Christ's kingdom on earth. Black people cannot build dignity on their knees worshipping a white Christ. We must put down this white Jesus

which the white man gave us in slavery and which has
been tearing us to pieces.[17]

The major contemporary proponent of Black Theology is Dr.
James H. Cone, professor of theology at Union Theological
Seminary in New York. His views are more consistent with
the "orthodox" doctrines of the Christian tradition, Black
or White. His pioneering work, *Black Theology and Black
Power,* broke new ground for Christian theologians in 1969.
Reactions to his views have been international in scope and
appreciation.

Cone sees the primary task of Black Theology to be that of
analyzing the nature of the gospel of Jesus Christ in light of
the oppression of Black people so that Black people will see
the gospel as inseparable from their oppressed condition.
This permits them to break the chains of oppression and hu-
miliation. It becomes, in fact, a theology of and for the Black
community.

Cone sees the central figure of Black Theology as *Jesus
Christ:*

> There can be no Christian theology which does not have
> Jesus Christ as its point of departure . . . unlike White the-
> ology which tends to make the Christ-event an abstract,
> intellectual idea, Black theology believes that the Black
> community itself is precisely where Christ is at work. . . .
> This is what God's revelation means to Black and White
> America, and why Black theology may be the only pos-
> sible theology in our time.[18]

For Cone, Black Theology confronts the racist nature of American society by stripping God of colorblindness. He states:

> To say God is color blind is analogous to saying that God
> is blind to justice and injustice, to right and wrong, to good
> and evil. . . . In the New Testament, Jesus is not *for all* but
> for the oppressed, the poor and unwanted of society, and
> against oppressors. The God of the biblical tradition is not

uninvolved or neutral regarding human affairs: rather he is quite involved. He is active in human history taking sides with the oppressed of the land.[19]
The emergence of Black Theology, as expressed by Cleage, Cone and others, indicates very clearly the present disillusionment and rejection by a significant number of Blacks with White "Christianity."[20] Black people by their rejection of "Christianity" are by that very act manifesting a search for the fulfillment of their spiritual needs.

In view of this a redefined Black people must evaluate the truth and reality of Christianity independent of White-racist definitions and expressions in institutions of oppression. Until Blacks can objectively examine and assess Christianity and its Christ in this way, their minds are still being controlled by the White world. In effect failure to do this would contradict the positive forces of Black consciousness as they have been described.

From our vantage point these Black theologians have gone a long way toward defining a Christianity independent of White thinking. However, nagging questions remain: Is there something more substantive to Christ than his color and his ability to identify with the Black community and fight its oppressors? Is the true nature of Christianity ever ultimately dependent on the expression of those who profess to be Christian? Is Christianity ever completely synonymous with human institutions? Is it possible for Blacks and Whites to have their spiritual needs met by one and the same God who affirms the humanity of both? We will examine these questions in the chapters to follow.

6
What Blacks Must Know about Christianity

We saw in the last chapter that Black consciousness enables Blacks to redefine their existence and role in a White-racist world. Black consciousness makes it possible for Blacks to view themselves as equals. It also confronts the White world with the reality of the personhood of Blacks and therefore makes it possible for Whites to be resensitized to their own humanity which has been obscured by the forces of White racism.

Black consciousness perceived in this way is the most creative and positive force operating in American society to bring the Black world and the White world together. If America is to survive as a nation and to realize the high ideal of the equal dignity and worth of all people and of their right to participate in a free society, Black consciousness must be recognized as a constructive force, not a destructive one.

America's greatness has always been tainted by its inability to express the equality and freedom of all of its people (especially its Black people). Black consciousness enables both Blacks and nonblacks to view themselves and each other as human and equal citizens. It thereby lays the foundation for the necessary restructuring of American institutions which will actualize freedom and equality, rather than oppression and discrimination.

We have seen that Black consciousness also lays the basis and creates the desire for a new Black religious experience and expression. Those who criticize and fear Black consciousness because of the implications of what religion should be for the new Black person fail to comprehend the potentially positive religious forces which Black consciousness precipitates.

Any person who hates himself has, in a very real sense, disqualified himself for an experience with God. Black consciousness seeks to destroy the negative self-concept and images (created in the White world and furthered by its institutions) that make Black people hate themselves and view themselves as less than human. These negative concepts are replaced with a positive self-image which affirms the full humanity of Blacks, the beauty of Blackness, the rich legacy of Black achievements and the potential of Blacks to control their own destinies. The theological basis for affirmation will be taken up later. Here it is enough to say that an independent sense of responsibility and worth helps people to accept their own strengths and weaknesses, achievements and failures.

It is absurd to confront oppressed people with a sense of guilt and wrong when they (by definition) are the objects of hate and exploitation and view themselves as innocent and powerless victims of oppression. To tell a Black person who is insensitive to his humanity that in order for him to have an experience with God he must confess his own guilt and wrong is, psychologically and historically, an insensitive display of religious creed.

Jesse B. Semple expressed the Black man's inability to accept his personal guilt, sin and damnation by saying that he knows he is going to heaven because he has already been in the hell of Harlem. As long as an individual can project or displace failure, apathy and social impotence to others, he is incapable of accepting full human responsibility. Such persons disqualify themselves from a complete and genuine experience with themselves and God. The subjective force of Black consciousness emancipates Blacks to accept the reality of their responsibility as human persons.

In addition to a sense of full human responsibility, the new Black person has a new potential to objectively evaluate the dominant issues that relate to his total being. One aspect of that being is "spiritual" needs. It is incumbent upon Black people to re-evaluate "Christianity," which they have justifiably seen as White, dehumanizing and oppressive. Throughout the Black protest against the Whiteness of Christianity, there were Blacks who consistently made the vital distinction between "Christianity" (as expressed and espoused by oppressors and their institutions) and Christianity (as an independent religious reality). Frederick Douglass concluded that his attack against Christianity, which we previously mentioned, was a charge against

the *slave-holding religion* of this land, and with no possible reference to Christianity proper; for, between the Christianity of this land, and the Christianity of Christ, *I recognize the widest possible difference*—so wide, that to receive the one as good, pure, and holy, is of necessity to reject the other as bad, corrupt, and wicked. . . . I love the pure perceivable and impartial Christianity of Christ: I

therefore hate the corrupt, slaveholding, women-whip-
ping, cradle-plundering, partial and hypocritical Christianity of this land. Indeed, I can see no reason, but the most
deceitful one, for calling the religion of this land Christianity. I look upon it as the climax of all misnomers, the
boldest of all frauds, and the grossest of all libels.[1]
Richard Allen and Absalom Jones, W. E. B. DuBois, Richard
Wright, James Baldwin, Malcolm X and James Cone all made
the vital distinction between what Christianity is in its racist
expression and what Christianity is and ought to be to all
who claim to be followers of Christ. Even Malcolm X in his
Autobiography shows his awareness of the independent reality of true Christianity.

> I would explain that it was our [the Muslims'] belief that
> Christianity did not perform what Christ taught. I never
> failed to cite that even Billy Graham, challenged in Africa,
> had himself made the distinction, "I believe in Christ, not
> Christianity."[2]

An awareness of this distinction between what Christianity
is and how Christianity *was used* in America against Blacks
enables us to conclude that the truth of Christianity cannot
be determined solely by its sociological expression in American history. There is reason for suspicion and hostility on the
part of Blacks; this has been demonstrated. But both the non-
Christian Black person and White people who desire to judge
Christianity must ask the elemental question: What is true
Christianity and how do I know it is true?

Blacks who want to think independently cannot allow
White "Christian" society, which has lied about and to
Blacks, to define the Christian faith. The White Americans
who have perverted history to exclude their own atrocities
and to ignore Black achievements also may have perverted
Christianity.

Those Blacks who reject the Christian God as too White and

too inseparably united to racist ideology and institutions must have this image destroyed if they are to have an experience with the *true* God. We have come to believe that the true God who can meet the total objective and subjective needs of all people is the God manifested in the historical person of Jesus Christ.

This realization in no way seeks to distract from or offset the fact that Black people have an irrefutable case against White "Christianity." But it is meant to emphasize that Black people, like all other people in our society, will never ultimately be satisfied and truly free until they have had a genuine redemptive experience with God who has made himself known in Jesus Christ.

We have shown that Black consciousness is a positive force operating among Blacks in that it resensitizes them to their humanity and their responsibility, and it allows them to objectively evaluate and deal with forces operating in their everyday world. However, Black consciousness, as we have described it, is not intended to meet the specific spiritual need that is common to all people for a right standing before a holy and loving God.

Because of the negative impressions that are prevalent, a significant number of Blacks doubt the ability of "Christianity" to meet this need. Every independently thinking Black person must examine the original source of the Christian religion and determine whether or not his need for a right standing with God is met by the Christian God—not the White God of racist "Christianity."

A Black person in quest of God must learn from other Blacks who are disillusioned with "Christianity" yet recognize that its relevance and truth cannot be determined by indirect sociological analyses. To discover what real Christianity teaches one must go back to the primary sources. This is analogous, for example, to discovering the real truth about any religious

or political movement. One examines the primary sources—
the holy books, the statements of philosophy, ethics, belief
and the promotional materials.

In approaching Christianity one must thoroughly scruti-
nize the Bible to determine what it actually teaches about
Blacks and their relationship to God and others.

If a Black person accepts the distinction between an ideology and the use of that ideology, he or she can understand
how the Bible was misused and distorted to justify the inhuman treatment of Blacks by Whites. In addition, if it can
be demonstrated that the White man's use of the Bible to justify his racism is spurious, then every free-thinking Black
ought to evaluate the Bible independently—free of White in-
timidation—as it pertains to race and to other universal aspects of the human dilemma.

Cursed by God?

The first chapter of this book demonstrated that the major
foundation for the support of slavery and White supremacy
was the biblical record of the "curse on Ham," erroneously
interpreted as a curse on Blacks. We also saw that the Bible
was interpreted by many Whites to sanction the "natural
order" of slavery. Paul's teachings about the slave/master
relationship were construed and presented to justify slavery
and to foster the docility that was a necessary attribute of the
"perfect slave." We would like to consider what in fact the
Bible does say about each of these teachings.

Genesis 9:18-27 has been used by many White-racists to
teach that Black people have been cursed by God to be in utter
subjection and slavery to nonblacks. This biblical incident
involves Noah, his three sons (Japheth, Ham and Shem) and
one of his grandsons, Canaan, the youngest son of Ham. After
the flood, Noah planted a vineyard and became drunk from
its wine. In his tent he lay uncovered and his son Ham saw

Noah's nakedness and told his two brothers, Shem and Japheth. These two sons took a robe, walked backward so that they would not see their father's nakedness, and covered the drunken Noah.

When Noah awoke and learned what had happened he spoke these words, "Cursed be Canaan; a slave of slaves shall he be to his brothers" (v. 25). Noah continued his prophecy with a comment about each son, repeating twice that Canaan is to be a slave to his brothers.

It is obvious from this passage that the curse pronounced by Noah is not upon Ham but upon Canaan. Therefore, in order to reconstruct what took place, whatever sinful act occurred and elicited Noah's curse, it cannot be ascribed to Ham, but to Canaan. The apparent contradiction between the fact that the text records that Ham "saw the nakedness of his father" and the fact that Canaan is cursed by Noah is adequately explained by an alternate meaning of "youngest son" in verse 24. It records that "when Noah awoke from his wine and knew what his youngest son had done to him," he pronounced the curse upon Canaan. But since Ham is not Noah's youngest son, the guilty party was another. The alternate meaning of "youngest son" is "grandson" which in this case would logically explain why the curse is upon Canaan, the grandson of Noah.[3]

Thus having established that Canaan and not Ham was the object of Noah's curse, it remains to be seen how the incident has been twisted to apply to Blacks. In order to apply "the curse" to Blacks the following propositions must be established in the text: (1) Blacks are descendents of Canaan; (2) Noah's words are valid as a curse; (3) the curse applies today; and (4) we should enforce the curse.

None of these are supported clearly by the teaching of the passage and the first is even strongly contradicted. The pronouncement, which is best understood as a prophecy, is not

applied to Ham but to Canaan, Ham's youngest son, and thus
it only could be applied to Canaan's descendants. The prog-
eny of Canaan are recorded in Genesis 10:15-19. It is clear
that they are not inhabitants of Africa and were not considered as black-skinned by those of the ancient world.[4] The
exegetical fact that Blacks are not descendants of Canaan is
enough to refute the arguments that Noah's prophecy applies
to Black people today. In addition, the prophecy seems to
have been fulfilled through the defeat of the Canaanites by
the children of Israel as recorded in the book of Joshua. This
victory, ordained by God as a judgment for sin, subdued the
Canaanites who were not killed (cf. Joshua 9:23 in regard to
the Gibeonites). Thus, if the curse is to be fulfilled today it
would apply to a small number of White descendants of Canaan who have not intermarried with descendants of Shem
and Japheth. The Bible does not teach that Black people are
reduced by God to an inferior status, but rather predicts judgment on the White Canaanites for their sins.

It should also be noted that the Bible actually does record
in Genesis 10 the contributions of those who are the indisputable progenitors of Blacks. To Ham's other sons, Cush,
Egypt and Put, are ascribed the earliest beginnings of great
human civilizations, such as Assyria, Babylon, Accad, Egypt
and Ethiopia.[5] In this respect the Bible demonstrates its honesty and objectivity in recording the accomplishments and
history of all ancient people.

Using race or color to justify the dominance of one person
or group over another is a characteristic of a racist mind. God,
as revealed in the Bible, is not governed by distinctions of
color. But our purposes in exposing the "colors" of Canaan
and his brothers is to show Black people, who live in a color-
conscious world, the absolute objectivity and integrity of a
book which has been mishandled and misrepresented by
White oppressors.

The Bible, the original source of Christian teaching, neither teaches nor supports the inhuman institution of slavery, especially in its barbarous American form.

The Bible and Slavery

One argument adduced to defend slavery asserted that slavery is a "natural" expression of God's will to introduce "illiterate," "uncivilized" Blacks to the benefits of White, Western civilization. This type of theological reasoning is absurd as a defense of slavery (or segregation). For example, one can say it is "natural" that corrupt men seeking personal gain should organize crime syndicates and provide a great source of enjoyment and release from frustration to a great mass of people. But does that mean it ought to be done? No. God has *allowed* it, but that does not mean he has *approved* it. This type of argument in defense of slavery or segregation fails to distinguish between what God approves and what God allows. God permits events to accomplish his will, but all that he permits is not according to his desires. God's providential will (i.e., what actually happens) does not equal his desired will. Slavery, therefore, cannot be attributed to the desired will of God, but to evil human desire for dominance and for personal gain.

A second type of proslavery argument is based upon biblical examples of slavery and segregation. The saying goes, "What God approved in the Old Testament and sanctioned in the New, cannot be sin." But do these examples support slavery and segregation in America? If everything which the Bible reports and God permitted was to be an example for us to follow, then polygamy, murder and divorce are God's express will for people today.[6] Jesus says in Matthew 19:8 that the Law of Moses allowed divorce because of man's "hardness of heart." There were provisions for divorce in the Old Testament, but Jesus said divorce is not part of God's desired

will because the principles of God's intent in creation are
against it. Likewise, the fact that there are examples of slavery in the Bible and provisions for certain aspects of it does
not mean that slavery is God's will.

A third biblical support for slavery and, indirectly, for
segregation uses the New Testament instructions for slaves
and masters.[7] Since most of these passages were written by
the Apostle Paul, he has been subjected to various verbal as-
saults and his teachings have been interpreted to serve as
the basis for a repudiation of Christianity. If Paul's teaching
is to be properly understood, the following points must be
considered: (1) Paul was not dealing with slavery identical
to slavery in America; (2) Paul dealt only with relations between slave and master *within* the Christian community;
(3) Paul's instructions actually undermined the whole institution of slavery; and (4) Paul espoused a body of teaching
which would make it *impossible* for Christians to institute a
system of slavery. We will look at each of these in turn.

Slavery in the Roman world of Paul's day was not founded
upon a system which assumed the superiority or inferiority
of a people *based on the color of their skin.* A person's servitude did not indicate innate lack of human worth and ca-
pabilities. Usually one became a slave because of forces of
circumstance, such as defeat in war or economic depriva-
tion. The slave in the Roman world had rights and privileges
which were not afforded to slaves in the United States, for example, rights of maintaining a family, legal recourse against
masters, rights of private ownership and the possibility of
being freed without permanent stigma [8] (The point here is
not to justify slavery *in any form* but only to highlight the
contrasts between the Roman and American types.) All too
often it has been assumed that slavery in the Roman world
was exclusively limited to Blacks. This explains why racist
minds could easily use Pauline passages to justify their treat-

ment of Blacks in America. But slavery in ancient Rome was not limited to any single ethnic group or class. It was possible for any man or woman to become a slave.

Second, Paul's message was addressed only to those masters and slaves who had received the gospel message and become Christians. The principles which he set forth were not meant to govern the larger society on the issue of slavery. These principles did not alter the privileges which a slave, Christian or not, had before Roman law. Thus if Pauline teaching regarding the obedience of slaves is to be applied to all Blacks, then all Blacks must by definition be Christians, and that runs counter to the assumption on which missions to Blacks were based.

Third, it is a historical fact that the principles which Paul taught concerning slave-master relations within the Christian community actually laid the foundation for the abolition of slavery.[9] Paul's principles, if examined closely, show that the relation between master and slave is based on human equality and mutual respect which are by nature incompatible with chattel racial slavery. Moreover, since in the Roman world slavery was basically a machine for social and economic organization, Paul's statement that masters should give to their slaves that which is "just and equal" would make it impossible for slavery to continue as a viable, profitable institution.[10]

Fourth, many who criticize Paul because he did not condemn slavery as it manifested itself in America fail to realize that he could not condemn that with which he was unfamiliar. Paul does teach principles which would condemn any who would create slave institutions and who, at the same time, call themselves Christians. This statement is not meant to judge or condemn all those in the past who called themselves Christians and held slaves; but it is meant to suggest that one has reason to suspect their true character.

The concept of human unity and worth based upon God's act of creation is a revolutionary idea. In addition, Paul's realistic teaching that all people are by nature evil and capable of dominating others argues for the eradication of slavery. Paul further teaches that in the Christian community racial, social and class distinctions are of no importance: "There is neither Jew nor Greek, there is neither slave nor free, there is neither male nor female; for you are all one in Christ Jesus" (Gal 3:28).

Having exposed the false nature of White-racist thought in their use of the Bible to justify the exploitation of Blacks in America, we can conclude that there is no such thing as a biblical curse on Blacks and no biblical basis to support slavery. If indeed a redefined Black person is capable of thinking independently of racist definitions and teachings, he or she must confess that the Bible must not be rejected as a book which gives Whites license to subjugate Blacks. The objectivity and honesty of the Bible in relationship to Black people has been demonstrated. What then does the Bible teach positively about Blacks (and humanity in general) in relation to God?

In God's Own Image

The Bible teaches that the universe and all within it has come into being by the will and action of a personal, triune God. The God of both the Old and New Testaments is the sovereign Creator-God who in the beginning created the heavens and the earth out of nothing. The Psalmist sang the praises of the Creator and stood in awe at his power:

Praise the LORD!
Praise the LORD from the heavens,
    praise him in the heights!
Praise him, all his angels,
    praise him, all his host!

Praise him, sun and moon,
  praise him, all you shining stars!
Praise him, you highest heavens,
  and you waters above the heavens!

Let them praise the name of the LORD!
  For he commanded and they were created.
And he established them for ever and ever;
  he fixed their bounds which cannot be passed.
  (Ps 148:1-6)

The prophets of the Old Testament likewise declared the reality of God as Creator (e.g., Is 40:25-29; Amos 4:13). Jesus, the self-confessed God-Man, assumed God as Creator when he spoke of God as the loving Father who providentially controlled the most insignificant aspects of the world (Mt 5:43-48; 10:29-31; Lk 12:7). At the end of the biblical canon the heavens cry in praise to God the Creator:
  Worthy art thou, our Lord and God,
  to receive glory and honor and power,
  for thou didst create all things,
  and by thy will they existed and were created. (Rev 4:11)
The meaning of the doctrine of creation, particularly as it is applied to Blacks in America today, centers in the biblical affirmation that "God saw everything that he had made, and behold, it was very good" (Gen 1:31). For the individual who knows the Creator-God, human existence is not meaningless. Despite the frustrations and evil of daily life, the creation itself and its movement in history is under the control of God's purposes. The creation account provides the basis for *meaning* in life for all people, Black and White.

Man is the focal point of God's creation. Man and woman were uniquely created by the direct activity of God. The Bible records that "God created man in his own image" (Gen 1:27) and that "the LORD God formed man of dust from the ground, and breathed into his nostrils the breath of life; and man became a living being" (Gen 2:7). Thus, God created man as an animated body like all other living beings, but in God's own image. This is not a White image or a Black image. Man is a "psycho-physical unity: both a body and a soul, completely and simultaneously."[11]

The fact that humanity is created in the image and likeness of God gives man the full potential and privilege of having intimate communion with the God who created him. And because of this "image of God" in man, no person can be fully satisfied until he or she experiences the reality of this personal relationship with God.

The most obvious application of the biblical teaching concerning the creation is that all people have equal value and dignity. God created one pair of humans from whom all men and women derive. They all equally possess the image of God because humanity is a unity—it came from a common source, Adam. The importance of this should not be overlooked because "the decision to promote equality of opportunity in the social order is an ethical decision and does not stand or fall according to whether scientists furnish indisputable proof that biological equality exists."[12] As an ethical decision, equality of treatment must have a legitimate foundation. Christian doctrine provides such a basis, relating equality directly to God's creative activity.

In addition to affirming the unity of humanity, the biblical teaching concerning creation also supports the worth of the individual and his right to survive. The individual must recognize that he or she is worthy of respect and dignity and possesses the right of survival. We have seen that Black consciousness as a positive psychological force among many Blacks asserts the dignity and worth of Blacks and of their right to survive. But it cannot be said to support it. The creation of man in the image and likeness of God becomes the support for this reality.

Perhaps one of the most beautiful expressions of the meaning of the creation of man is found in this adaptation from the Talmud:

Why did God create only one Adam and not many at a time?

He did this to demonstrate that one man in himself is an entire universe. Also He wished to teach mankind that he who kills one human being is as guilty as if he had destroyed the entire world. Similarly, he who saves the life of one single human being is as worthy as if he had saved all humanity.

God created only one man so that people should not try to feel superior to one another and boast of their lineage in this wise: "I am descended from a more distinguished Adam than you."

He also did this so that the heathen should not be able to say that since many men had been created at the same time, it was conclusive proof that there was more than one God.

Lastly, He did this in order to establish His own power and glory. When a maker of coins does his work he uses only one mould and all the coins emerge alike. But the King of Kings, blessed be His Name, has created all mankind in the mould of Adam, and even so no man is identical to another. For this reason each person must respect himself and say with dignity: "God created the world on my account. Therefore, let me not lose eternal life because of some vain passion!"[13]

The Bible records the rebellion of man through the sin of Adam which broke the fellowship with God. It teaches that each individual born since that rebellious act has inherited the evil nature of his predecessor, Adam, and thus by nature rebels and revolts against the will of the God-Creator. The penalty for this revolt is death—separation from God—which climaxes in "the punishment of eternal destruction and exclusion from the presence of the Lord and from the glory of his might" (2 Thess 1:9).

God, however, has acted graciously toward us by doing for us what we could not do for ourselves. God himself became a man. And though he partook of human nature he did not sin. "The Word became flesh" (Jn 1:14) and shared the struggles of humanity. Jesus Christ, the eternal Son of God, "knew himself to be a man" and suffered temptation, weariness, hunger and thirst and all the joys and sorrows of common humanity (Heb 2:17-18). "His whole manner of life was genuinely human."[14] Yet he was God come "in the likeness of sinful flesh [humanity]" so that he might condemn "sin in the flesh [his body]" (Rom 8:3) in order to bring forgiveness to all who turn to him in repentance and trust. When God became man, he entered the world as the son of a poor family living in a despised and persecuted nation. He did not identify himself with earthly royalty and riches, though he was King of kings, but identified himself with humility and poverty.

The Example of Christ

The character of God as revealed in the earthly life of the God-Man, Jesus Christ, displays qualities which speak to the modern tensions existing between Blacks and Whites. Jesus revealed the character of God by word and deed.

A primary theme of his teaching was the kingdom of God. By this he did not mean an earthly, secular kingdom which would be like the nations of the earth. Rather, he stressed that the kingdom was realized in the lives of people who submitted themselves to God. This kingdom finds expression *within history*, in the lives of those who submit to God's will, and its full and future expression in the earthly reign of the King himself who returns to establish it.

Although there are futuristic aspects to the kingdom, the important point is that God's power and love are to be manifested in the lives of those who accept Christ's rule. This present aspect of the kingdom of God thus affirms the dignity, value and right to survival of all people, either as actual or as potential members of that kingdom. It is not an act of sociopolitical suicide for any person to submit his life to Christ as Lord and Savior. It is an act of affirmation of life.

In this connection we must clarify an important point. The popular understanding of Jesus' principle of "turning the other cheek" implies that a Christian simply acquiesces to forces of harm and destruction (Mt. 5:39). We believe this is an erroneous interpretation. We must distinguish between suffering for righteousness' sake (by virtue of identification with Christ) and suffering because of injustice.

When persecuted for the sake of the gospel, Christians have a responsibility to "turn the other cheek." But it is incumbent upon every person, created in the image of God, to resist unjust forces that threaten survival.

Since the turn-the-other-cheek principle has been misinterpreted by many "Christians" to justify the totally nonviolent response of Black people to institutions of oppression, many Blacks have come to view Christianity as incompatible with Black survival. This is blasphemy!

Black people, like all other people in society, possess within the deepest levels of their personalities the principle of survival that originates from God himself. The same principle that operates when Whites protect themselves and their families from armed burglars makes it necessary for Blacks to respond to White police brutality in ways which will enable them to survive. It means that a Black man whose family is being harassed by White teen-agers will respond to protect himself and his family. This principle means that Black parents who recognize the inequities of the educational system which teaches their children will respond to eliminate those inequities.

Nevertheless, the *guiding* principle of life for those who consider themselves members of Christ's present kingdom (that is, those who call themselves Christian) consists of loving obedience to God and loving concern for other people. Jesus himself summed up the revealed will of God in these two great commandments: "You shall love the Lord your God with all your heart, and with all your soul, and with all your mind. This is the great and first commandment. And a second is like it, You shall love your neighbor as yourself" (Mt 22:37-38). These commandments, which only Jesus has perfectly fulfilled, obviously exclude all elements of racism and discrimination.

Not only did Jesus' teaching concerning the ethic of the kingdom of God challenge bigotry and prejudice, but his actions did likewise. One of the most despised "racial" groups of New Testament times were the Samaritans. The Jews hated the Samaritans, who were "half-Jewish," because they considered the Samaritans to be religious heretics. Jesus, while recognizing their religious errors, did not despise the Samaritans. While traveling through Samaria, Jesus met an adulterous woman at Jacob's well (Jn 4:1-42). He spoke with her because he recognized her dignity as a person created by God. Jesus kindly led her to see her need of spiritual life and to recognize him as the Sent One of God.

Also, one of Jesus' most famous parables, the parable of the good Samaritan, is a damning indictment of the hypocrisy and bigotry of Jesus' contemporaries. The hero is a Samaritan. That parable, which is found in Luke 10:25-37, describes the plight of a man who was beaten and robbed on the highway. A priest and a Levite both see the man and comprehend his situation but do nothing. Only the Samaritan stops to help the man and care for his wounds. The Samaritan, whom

Jesus' countrymen despised, was the only one who showed mercy to the injured man and sacrificed on his behalf. The neighbor-love which Jesus taught is not limited by bigotry and prejudices.[15] If Jesus were telling that story in America today, the hero would probably be Black.

Jesus' final action to demonstrate his repudiation of racism and discrimination was the sacrifice of his life for the world's guilt. Indeed, the primary purpose of God's becoming a man and sharing human suffering was to die for the selfishness, bigotry, discrimination, inhumanity and rebellion of *all* people who put their trust in him, regardless of their economic, political, social or racial status. His death on the cross is applicable on equal terms of faith and repentance to all people. Jesus said that he "came not to be served but to serve, and to give his life as a ransom [payment for sin] for many" (Mk 10:45). It is clear from Jesus' command to his apostles to "Go therefore and make disciples of all nations ... " (Mt 28:19) that Jesus died for people of *all* races and nations.

On the basis of redemption in Jesus Christ, any group that calls itself *Christian* and discriminates against a race or class is simply rejecting the biblical pattern. The New Testament church was not composed of nice, ticky-tacky, White middle-class people.[16] Rather, the unity of faith overcame the social and racial barriers which were present. The meek and mild, White, Nordic Jesus is phony—at best a product of ignorant ethnocentrism, at worst of White racism. Jesus is not the God of White people; he is the God of the universe and his death for the rebellion of this world applies to people of all races.[17]

If you want to be a Christian, you must personally trust Jesus Christ as Savior from personal sin and commit yourself to Christ as Lord in your daily life. Christianity is Christ —Christ who has died, risen and ascended into heaven to provide full forgiveness and power to those who follow him. Black consciousness as a subjective psychological force can

never give individuals the completeness of life and whole-
ness of personality that is available through fellowship with
God as revealed in Jesus Christ.

We have seen in this chapter the vital factors that must
ultimately govern our response to Christianity. First, we
have seen the positive contribution of Black consciousness.
That movement has helped Blacks to redefine themselves
independent of racist categories. It has provided Blacks with
a sense of responsibility and a reason for looking again at
the claims of Christianity.

Second, we have seen that true, biblical Christianity must
be distinguished from the "Christianity" manifested by im-
perfect, racist society in America.

Third, we have examined the Bible to see if there is any
support there for the subjugation of Blacks by Whites. We
have found not only that there is no biblical support for slavery or segregation, but also that the Bible teaches the full
equality and worth of all people. All people were created in
the image of God from a common ancestor—Adam. Our
equality and worth was most supremely manifested when
the self-confessed God-Man, Jesus Christ, offered his life to
bring forgiveness to all who trust in him, regardless of their
racial or social status. If we commit ourselves to Christ as
God, he offers us forgiveness and fullness of life which does
not negate our identity nor force us to surrender to a hostile
environment.

Therefore, Blacks who now reject the Christ of true Christianity cannot do so because of Jesus' "Whiteness" and his
supposed association with forces of oppression. Rather, that
rejection can only be based on an individual's refusal to accept a Christ who challenges him or her to face his human
inadequacies, failures and guilt. That is a refusal to accept
a Jesus who is willing and able to enter into the struggle of
Black people in White America.

7

What White Christians Must Do with Their Churches

Despite the emphasis in the last chapter, we do not believe that the racial problems in America can be solved by Blacks alone. Racism in America is basically a White problem: White society created it and keeps it going through its institutions. If institutions reflect the attitudes and values of people, then the most ideal and humane way for Whites to eliminate institutional racism is for them to change their attitudes about Blacks, and then restructure and reorganize their institutions so that they are no longer oppressive. However, the deep-seated nature of White racism makes it imperative that in some cases structural change precede attitudinal change if oppression of Blacks is to be quickly and effectively eliminated.

Whites must begin to view Blacks as human beings endowed with the same rights and privileges as White people. Nonetheless, our discussion of Black consciousness has demonstrated the inability of Whites to make this change apart from Black assertiveness and confrontation.

In this chapter we would like to suggest ways in which the White Christian community, both individually and corporately, can act in order for greater justice and equality to be realized and for the Black person's negative impressions of Christianity to be altered.

We have demonstrated that "Christianity" has been and continues for the most part to be inextricably bound to racist institutions. "The white church as an institution has not only been supported by but has also given *its sanction* to the other major institutions of the society—business, education and government."[1] It cannot be too strongly emphasized that Christianity as an institution (regardless of theological refinements or denominational distinctions) is the major force in undergirding and approving the values of the socio-political and economic institutions of America. Peter Berger in analyzing the relationship of Christianity to American institutions concludes that "commitment to Christianity . . . undergoes a fatal identification with commitment to society, to respectability, to the American way of life."[2] The most dramatic expression of this identification in recent years has been the Moral Majority and similar conservative political movements which have identified themselves as Christian.

Just as the White church has supported and continues to support oppressive forces by both its action and inaction, we believe that the White church, recognizing its true identity as God's people who should function as a force for good, can generate and advance those values which liberate and promote justice for all Americans. The inability of the White Christian church to demonstrate values which oppose racist forces has made the church ineffective in aiding Black people (and others) in their quest for survival.

We hesitate to offer prepackaged solutions to the racial problem. Today's solutions may become tomorrow's problems. Only active, daily involvement can be fruitful in judging the feasibility of any proposed solution.

To those who insist upon detailed and concrete plans of action, . . . [we] can only urgently advise them to consult their congressman, their psychoanalyst, or better still, if they are determined believers, their local priest. . . . [We] can take this facetious method of answering with a good conscience because . . . [we are] convinced that we all, deep in our hearts, *know exactly what to do*, though most of us would rather die than do it.[3]

Changing Attitudes

Because racism is a multiheaded monster, its destruction demands a diversity of responses, programs and solutions. Individuals who commit themselves to the abolition of racism must deal initially with their own racist attitudes and fears. If they do not, they will merely help further racism, not abolish it.

Those who call themselves Christian (in the biblical sense) must *repent* of any attitudes that give them a sense of superiority over other people because of race (see Jas 2:8-9; 1 Jn 1:9-10). The beginning of the elimination of White racism is the admission of shared guilt: the admission that I am wrong, that I have offended, that I have benefited from a society that assumes I am superior because I am White and the Black person is inferior because he is Black.

White persons who say, "I never owned slaves" or "I never raped a Black woman" or "I did not kill Dr. King" or "I have not opposed affirmative action programs" or "I have not opposed open housing" are escaping their own guilt. That guilt is the guilt of ignorance, the guilt of insensitivity to the cry and struggle of Black people, the guilt of omission which refuses to stop the continued oppression and domination of Blacks (and others) by Whites.

What white Americans have never fully understood—but
what . . . [Blacks] can never forget—is that the white society is deeply implicated in the ghetto [the epitome of the
oppression of Blacks]. White institutions created it, white
institutions maintain it, and white society condones it.[4]
This full admission of wrong does not in any way destroy the
reality of a White person's humanity. Part of the White-racist
mental pathology is that Whites cannot admit their guilt in
oppressing Blacks because in their thinking a "superior people" can do no wrong. Because of this, many Whites view
slavery as the benign introduction of Blacks to the benefits
of Western civilization. They also view segregation and subordination as desirable for Blacks.

We believe, however, that White persons who admit their
ignorance and guilt and confront their fears are, in actuality,
affirming their humanity, because they view themselves as
creatures capable of both good and evil. Still, this realization should not be viewed as an "if-then" argument. That is,
Whites cannot escape their own guilt by saying that Blacks,
being human, would have done the same thing if they had
had the opportunity.

The fact is that *Whites have created and maintained* institutions which commit atrocities against Blacks for which all
Whites (either directly or indirectly, consciously or unconsciously) share a responsibility.

The present-day affirmative action approach to inequality
of opportunity is, in our opinion, but one of a myriad of Black
initiatives which Christians should support against White-
racist institutions. However, White Christians should not
conclude that such support of legitimate Black claims can
compensate for the atrocities committed by White "Christianity" against Blacks. A simple commitment to affirmative
action is too easy an option for Whites to exercise to remove
their guilt about "the Black problem" and to minimize their

personal and institutional involvement. Giving a few jobs and minor subcontracts to a few Blacks is not enough. White Christians who participate in and significantly benefit from the greatest economy the world has ever known must involve Blacks in all aspects of their institutions (including churches) and businesses so that Blacks are given more than the monetary crumbs of American wealth and power.

While a meaningful affirmative action is one proper response, the complexity of White racism and its effects, as abetted by the forces of "Christianity," demands that White Christians not only give of their nonhuman resources but also of themselves to help restructure our society. Forceful action must take place on all levels, not simply to erase guilt but to revamp American society so that Blacks can participate as political, economic and human equals. In addition, Blacks will not simply wait for White churches to respond to their legitimate demands but will continue to initiate in all areas those programs and policies which will give Blacks actual power bases.

We have met many Whites who have cried and wept as they have admitted their own racism but who have not truly repented: their actions (or lack of them) belie the change which they claim to have made. The last group that will help eradicate racism in America are Whites who simply weep and wail about their guilt. A change of attitude, based upon the admission of wrong must, in order to be valid, issue in change of action (2 Cor 7:8-10). Specifically, in whatever ways necessary, Whites must actively support Blacks in their survival struggle against institutional racism as manifested in housing, employment, financing and other forms of discrimination.

New Actions
Some Christians do not feel that they or their churches should

be involved in the socio-political problems created by White racism. Many believe that social concerns divert the church from its true mission—evangelism. Of course, the message of the kingdom of God must be spread so that people can come to a personal relationship with Christ. "Repentance and forgiveness of sins should be preached in his name to all nations" (Lk 24:47). And some Whites say that anything, which competes with or diverts them from preaching the good news of Jesus Christ is categorically wrong.

But this objection is founded on the false assumption that Christians may *either* preach the good news *or* work to improve social conditions. This is a false dichotomy: It is not a matter of either/or, but both/and. Jesus did not endorse a dichotomy between physical and spiritual ministries. The first chapter of the Gospel of Mark records that the activities of Jesus, apparently in the same day, included teaching in the synagogue, casting out evil spirits and healing many sick people. The compassion of Jesus moved him to minister to whole persons. Christians, who must be like Jesus, should not separate spiritual and social needs. Just as works without faith is dead, "so faith by itself, if it has no works, is dead" (Jas 2:17).

Since God commands Christians to "do good to all men" (Gal 6:10) and to be "careful to apply themselves to good deeds" (Tit 3:8), then we are disobedient if we do not show social concern in overt action. The Great Commission commands us to "make disciples of all nations, baptizing them in the name of the Father and of the Son and of the Holy Spirit, *teaching them to observe all that I have commanded you*" (Mt 28:19-20, italics ours). And the teaching of Jesus includes that children of the kingdom should be perfect as their heavenly Father is perfect, who does good to all people and sends sun and rain upon the evil and the good (Mt 5:43-48).

Christians should therefore be taught to *do* those actions

which promote the good of all. Christians should act on behalf of justice and righteousness in the social and political spheres and not neglect proclaiming salvation through the reconciling death of the God-Man, Jesus Christ. The example of Christ means that Christians must be involved in ministering to the whole person. It is inconceivable for Christians to say that they love others if they do not attack those forces which destroy them.

Other White Christians object that attempts to solve social problems are futile because, by nature, social problems are insoluble. This, however, is not a genuine objection to Christian involvement with social problems and social change since no one assumes that the problems can finally and completely be solved. In light of this fact, which is further illuminated by the biblical insight concerning the sinfulness of human nature, Christian social action must be absolutely realistic. If social evils will never be completely removed in this age, it does not follow that they cannot or should not be minimized *as much as possible*.[5] The Christian church is not responsible for success; it is responsible for obedience to the will of God who desires righteousness and justice in social, political and economic affairs.[6]

White Christians also object: "You can't legislate love. White people will be prejudiced against Blacks no matter how many laws are passed." But the goal of Christian social action is not to make people love one another but to stop them from expressing their hatred in overt individual and institutional ways that oppress other people. Penalties for murder do not eliminate the evil desire to murder, but they may discourage the act. Likewise, legal measures taken against racial discrimination attempt to change the action, not the attitude In addition, studies have shown that *law does change attitude*. Thus the very objection is false.[7]

A final objection to Christian social action is that it com-

promises the Christian faith. That is to say, the Christian faith
is compromised when it cooperates with non-Christians. But
this objection fails to take into account the fact that such cooperation takes place every day without compromise of the
Christian faith. Christians drive on the right side of the road
just like non-Christians; Christians pay taxes just like non-
Christians; they write letters to congressmen, vote for president and register their dogs, just like non-Christians and in
mutual agreement with non-Christians.

The issue of cooperation with non-Christians really concerns the level of cooperation. Most Christians believe that
it would be wrong to cooperate religiously with non-Christians as if there were no differences between them. The Bible
teaches that that is indeed correct (2 Cor 6:14—7:1). But in
matters of common interest which do not involve necessary
endorsement of a common religious position, the Bible indicates that we can and sometimes *should* cooperate with
non-Christians (see, for example, Rom 13:1-7; 1 Cor 5:9-13).

Conflict no doubt will arise, and perhaps there will be fric-
tions because of the good news of Jesus Christ. But these are
not reasons for avoiding involvement. In fact, noninvolve-
ment or so-called neutrality is a social position. It "conveys,
implicitly, an endorsement of the status quo. It puts one into
the position of seeming to bless or sanctify evil leaders, institutions, and practices instead of exposing and condemning the works of evil."[8] Neutrality also implies that the message of the church is "totally irrelevant to practical problems
except, perhaps, as it might change the motivations and aspirations of individuals who respond to it."[9]

Therefore, in light of biblical support for Christian involvement on behalf of the good of *whole* persons, we believe that
it is the proper mission of the Christian church to actively
support leadership and programs working both to destroy
the forces of institutional racism and to create a society in

which the justice of God is realized in human institutions.[10]

We would like to add a more *personal* interpretation of the Christian obligation to support efforts to eradicate racism. As noted in chapter five, we share a belief that Christ is committed to the oppressed and to their liberation. It is our opinion that these issues have been settled by the Scriptures and the life of Christ. Therefore, anyone who is truly Christian will be committed to the struggle with and for the oppressed. This commitment and involvement is the fulfillment of the biblical text that "you will know them by their fruits" (Mt 7:16, 20).

This active support may take on many forms. In one instance financial support may be primary: for example, money for the building of Black community enterprises. In another instance, an individual Christian or organization of Christians may join in active cooperation with others: for example, local pressure groups for Black inclusion in trade unions and local educational control. In other instances, Christians may provide leadership to programs which seek to promote racial justice and harmony: for example, educating *Whites* in the larger society at all levels concerning the need for social and attitudinal change.

Two positive examples of Black Christian organizations which have developed programs for Black liberation and which have received a measure of support from a few White churches are Urban Ministries, Incorporated of Chicago and Voice of Calvary Ministries in Mississippi. Urban Ministries, headed by the Rev. Melvin Banks, is a Black institution which spun off from the White organization Scripture Press.[11] It produces Sunday-school literature and other materials which are urban and Black-oriented for use in the Black community. It has met with growing appreciation and use by a number of Black churches and denominations, thus filling a real need for relevant, indigenous, biblical literature.

Voice of Calvary Ministries, founded and directed by the
Rev. John Perkins, is a tremendously significant, Black-led
Christian ministry.[12] Its wholistic approach to life includes
individual evangelism and Bible study, economic coopera-
tives, thrift shops, health clinics, day care and educational
alternatives including a school for the study of social change.
Perkins insists, as we do, upon the costly identification with
the oppressed in the name of Christ. Voice of Calvary's interracial staff, headed and directed by Blacks, is an example of
reconciliation and cooperation for concrete social change in
the heart of Mississippi's "closed society."

Challenge to the Churches

The ability of the Christian church as a major institutional
force to accomplish this kind of social change should not
be minimized. The historical role of Christianity has been
shown to be a primary force determining the normative values of our society—a society which is manifestly racist. If
Christian institutions were used effectively to support racist
values and institutions, how much more should they now
effectively support and create values and institutions which
recognize the dignity and equality of all races?

The White Christian church which has realized its responsibility to work actively to destroy racism often does not recognize that the very inner structure of its own church may
maintain policies and attitudes that contribute to the racism
it seeks to destroy. Just as we noted in chapter three that the
racism of society today has taken on a subtle and evasive
form in respect to its oppression of Blacks, so the racism of
the White church is difficult to fully isolate and identify.
However, as one focuses upon the inner structures of the
White Christian church, one can see features, programs and
attitudes which are racist.

For example, the curricula of the White church, despite

some cosmetic changes, primarily represents the world as White. They tell the receivers of their messages that all that is significant in this world and the world to come is White. It would appear to church members that God lives in the suburbs, has an occasional Black member or friend, fights crabgrass, has middle-class values and is White. These attitudes, impressions and values when transferred to the larger society lead individuals to believe that God is not concerned with the everyday oppression of Blacks and that the ghettos are the products of Black ignorance, laziness and immorality.

Another way in which the inner structure of the White church perpetuates racism is by investing and spending its monies and resources on enterprises which directly or indirectly exploit the Black community or which deny Blacks equal opportunity in employment, housing and education. White church organizations and leadership continue to unofficially support national and local political leadership that has been identified with conservative policies for solving race problems.

But probably the greatest support that the White church gives to racist institutions is its lack of commitment to Black organizations which are trying to alleviate the oppression of Blacks. For example, it appears that the policy of most White churches is not to speak out against the savage murder and beatings of Black people by policemen; not to speak out against the revival of the Ku Klux Klan and other White hate groups; not to use their influence to change deplorable housing conditions; and not to use their influence to change the "Whiteness" of their local schools.

Yet another evidence of racism within the White church is the overwhelming tendency to flee when Blacks move into the neighborhood. The justifications given usually camouflage the real reason for the flight: the fear of Black men having sexual relations with White women. The origin of that fear has been described in chapter three. It is tragic that such fears and perversions run rampant, both consciously and unconsciously, among White people, even those who claim to be followers of Christ.

Yet another evidence of White racism in the White church is the refusal of White Christians to accept Black leadership which will not compromise with racism in any form and which challenges the status quo. Most White churches will pick and support black-skinned individuals (Negroes) who are the least threatening to the church's real position on issues relative to race. The White church which has come to view Black consciousness as a positive force in America cannot afford to delude itself in selecting Black leadership. It can only properly *recognize* Black leadership!

Though admittedly we have not isolated all the manifestations of attitudinal and structural racism within the White Christian church, we believe that those aspects which we have named provide adequate opportunities for White involvement in the elimination of racism.

To those White Christians who invariably ask, "What can we do?" we say without equivocation, "De-honkify (de-whiten) your church; its curriculum, its investment, its purchasing programs, its personnel, its leadership and its attitudes."

This type of action will not and cannot be a passive, gradual program. The racist attitudes and actions of the Christian church must be forcefully attacked, producing vigorous confrontation that should eventually result in the desired structural and attitudinal changes. James Baldwin says it so well: "The subtle and deadly change of heart that might occur in you would be involved with the realization that a civilization is not destroyed by wicked people: it is not necessary that people be wicked but only that they be spineless." Only a genuine, active social involvement will afford the White

Christian church the opportunity to become that positive sociological expression of Christianity which will aid Blacks in their re-evaluation and assessment of the true person and work of Jesus Christ.

To those White Christians who would ask for more concrete instruction on what to do, we reiterate Richard Wright's words: "We all, deep in our hearts, *know exactly what to do,* though most of us would rather die than do it."

Notes

Introduction
[1]James H. Cone and Gayraud S. Wilmore, eds., *Black Theology: A Documentary History, 1966-1979.*

Chapter 1: Christianity and Slavery
[1]John Pope-Hennessy, *Sins of the Fathers: A Study of the Atlantic Slave Traders, 1441-1807* (New York: Alfred A. Knopf, 1968), p. 8.

[2]*Ibid.,* p. 12.

[3]Frank Tannenbaum, *Slave & Citizen* (New York: Random House, 1946), p. 32. Tannenbaum also notes that many Africans lost their lives and never reached the New World. Of the total some have said "one-third of the Negroes taken from their homes died on the way to the coast and at embarkation stations, and that another one-third died crossing the ocean and in seasoning, so that only one-third finally survived to become the laborers and colonizers of the New World" (pp. 28-29).

[4]John Hope Franklin, *From Slavery to Freedom: A History of Negro Americans*, 3rd ed. (New York: Alfred A. Knopf, 1967), p. 59.

[5]Stanley M. Elkins, *Slavery: A Problem in American Institutional and Intellectual Life* (New York: Grosset and Dunlap, 1959), p. 99.

[6]Pope-Hennessy, pp. 97-116, describes briefly the conditions of the Middle Passage.

[7]Elkins outlines this "shock theory" and compares it to the concentration camps of World War 2, thus generating considerable debate. Elkins also compares British-American slavery with the slavery of Latin America, as does Tannenbaum, and contends that the Latin system possessed "a fluidity that permitted a transition

from slavery to freedom that was smooth, organic, and continuing" (p. 79). Cf. David B. Davis, *The Problem of Slavery in Western Culture* (Ithaca: Cornell Univ. Press, 1966), pp. 223-61, and Sidney Mintz, Review of *Slavery: A Problem in American Institutional and Intellectual Life* by Stanley Elkins, in *American Anthropologist* 63 (June 1961): 579-87.

[8]Winthrop D. Jordon, *White Over Black: American Attitudes Toward the Negro, 1550-1812* (Chapel Hill: Univ. of North Carolina Press, 1968), p. 73. This is a thorough, careful, scholarly work.

[9]W. E. Burghardt DuBois, *The World and Africa: An Inquiry into the Part Which Africa Has Played in World History* (New York: International Pub., 1946), p. 20.

[10]Jordon, p. 98.

[11]Carter G. Woodson, *The History of the Negro Church*, 2nd ed. (Washington: Associated Publishers, 1921), p. 2.

[12]Davis, p. 209.

[13]*Ibid.*, p. 205.

[14]Oscar Handlin, *Race and Nationality in American Life*, Anchor Books (Garden City, N.Y.: Doubleday, 1957), p. 14.

[15]Davis, pp. 204-5.

[16]Woodson, pp. 19-20.

[17]Joseph R. Washington, Jr., *Black Religion: The Negro and Christianity in the United States* (Boston: Beacon Press, 1964), p. 181. This work, in addition to summarizing historical data, provides a theological analysis of Christianity and Black Americans.

[18]William Warren Sweet, *The Story of Religion in America*, rev. and enlarged ed. (New York: Harper and Bro., 1950), p. 168.

[19]Kenneth M. Stampp, *The Peculiar Institution: Slavery in the Ante-Bellum South* (New York: Random House, 1956), p. 158, italics ours.

[20]*Ibid.*

[21]That this "proper instruction" was consistent and effective is witnessed by these words of a North Carolina bondsman recorded in the 1840s and quoted in Gilbert Osofsky, ed., *The Burden of Race: A Documentary History of Negro-White Relations in America* (New York: Harper and Row, 1966), p. 35: "On Sabbath there was one sermon preached expressly for the colored people. I became quite familiar with the texts. 'Servants be obedient to your masters.' 'Not with eye service as man pleasers.' 'He that knoweth his master's will and doeth it not, shall be beaten with many stripes,' and others of this class. . . . The first commandment impressed upon our minds was to obey our masters, and the second was . . . to do as much work when they or the overseers were not watching us as when they were." Osofsky's work has a sermon illustrating these principles on pages 39-44.

[22]Stampp, p. 161.

[23]*Ibid.*, p. 148.

[24]*Ibid.*, p. 71.

[25]William H. Grier and Price M. Cobbs, *Black Rage* (New York: Bantam Books, 1968), pp. 68-69, 71, italics ours.

[26]J. Oliver Buswell III, *Slavery, Segregation and Scripture* (Grand Rapids, Mich.: Eerdmans, 1964), p. 12. This work demonstrates that the same four categories of arguments are being used today to defend segregation.

[27]Ralph L. Moellering, *Christian Conscience and Negro Emancipation* (Philadelphia: Fortress Press, 1965), p. 50.

[28]*Ibid.*

[29]Osofsky, p. 93.

[30]Buswell, pp. 16-18. See also Charles E. Silberman, *Crisis in Black and White* (New York: Random House, 1964), pp. 172-74. Our rebuttal to this spurious argumentation is included in a later chapter.

[31]H. Shelton Smith, Robert T. Handy, and Lefferts A. Loetscher, *American Christianity: An Historical Interpretation with Representative Documents* (New York: Charles Scribner's Sons, 1963), 1:180.

[32]*Ibid.*

[33]William Warren Sweet, *Religion in the Development of American Culture: 1765-1840* (New York: Charles Scribner's Sons, 1952), p. 279.

[34]Smith et al., p. 293.

[35]*Ibid.*, p. 465.

[36]Gilbert Hobbs Barnes, *The Antislavery Impulse: 1830-1844* (New York: Harcourt, Brace and World, 1964), p. 12. This work caused debate upon its first issue in 1933 by demonstrating that revivalism, especially in the North and the West, contributed greatly to the Abolitionist Movement. Concerning Finney, though he was not an abolitionist agitator, he nevertheless strongly opposed slavery. Cf. Walter Unger, *The Social Views of Charles Grandison Finney*, unpublished Masters thesis, Trinity Evangelical Divinity School, 1969.

[37]Osofsky, pp. 87-88.

[38]Moellering, p. 70. Barnes's work is *An Inquiry into the Scriptural Views of Slavery* (Philadelphia: Perkins and Purves, 1846).

[39]Sweet, *The Story of Religion*, p. 291.

Chapter 2: Christianity and Segregation

[1]John Hope Franklin, "The Two Worlds of Race: A Historial View" in *The Negro American*, ed. Talcott Parsons and Kenneth B. Clark (Boston: Beacon Press, 1964), p. 53.

[2]Kenneth M. Stampp, *The Era of Reconstruction, 1865-1877* (New York: Random House, 1965), pp. 79-80.

[3]A good introduction to this debate is *Reconstruction in the South*, ed. Edwin C. Rozwene (Boston: D. C. Heath and Company, 1952) which is one of the books from the excellent *Problems in American Civilization* series. It contains selections which represent the traditional ("Southern") view and the revisionist view. In addition, E. Merton Coulter in *The South During Reconstruction, 1865-1877* (Vol. III of *A History of the South*, ed. Wendell Holmes Stephenson and E. Merton Coulter [Baton Rouge: Lousiana State Univ. Press, 1947]) supports the traditionalist interpretation. However, Kenneth M. Stampp, *The Era of Reconstruction* and John Hope Franklin, *Reconstruction After the Civil War*, The Chicago History of American Civilization, ed. Daniel J. Boorstin (Chicago: University of Chicago Press, 1961), seem to have dealt more accurately with the data as they presented their "revisionist" view. For a brief introduction to this problem see Arnold M. Rose, "Distortion in the History of American Race Relations" in *Assuring Freedom to the Free: A Century of Emancipation in the U. S. A.*, ed. Arnold M. Rose (Detroit:

Wayne State Univ. Press, 1964), pp. 27-44.

[4]Stampp, Era of Reconstruction, p. 110.

[5]Ibid., p. 129, italics ours.

[6]Ibid., pp. 134-35.

[7]Franklin, From Slavery to Freedom, p. 327.

[8]Ibid., p. 329.

[9]There is also recent considerable debate as to the origins of segregation. Joel Williamson, ed., The Origins of Segregation, Problems in American Civilization (Boston: Heath and Company, 1968), provides the best compilation and suggestions for further reading. C. Vann Woodward's The Strange Career of Jim Crow, 2nd ed. (New York: Oxford University Press, 1966), presents the view that segregation in the South is a relatively late phenomenon. In all of these discussions the gradual and varied nature of segregation should be emphasized.

[10]Woodward, p. 6.

[11]Report of the National Advisory Commission on Civil Disorders, Otto Kerner, Chairman (New York: Bantam Books, 1968), p. 215.

[12]Sweet, The Story of Religion in America, p. 317. The information for the present section is taken from Sweet's chapter, "The Churches North and South," pp. 312-26.

[13]Ibid., p. 325.

[14]Ibid., p. 327.

[15]Winthrop S. Hudson, Religion in America (New York: Charles Scribner's Sons, 1965), p. 203.

[16]Ibid., p. 217.

[17]David M. Reimers, White Protestantism and the Negro (New York: Oxford Univ. Press, 1965), p. 25, italics ours.

[18]Hudson, p. 221.

[19]Sweet, The Story of Religion, p. 329.

[20]Ibid., pp. 329-30.

[21]Robert T. Handy, "Negro Christianity and American Church Historiography" in Essays in Divinity, Reinterpretation in American Church History, vol. 5 (Chicago: Univ. of Chicago Press, 1968), pp. 95ff.

[22]Leonard Broom and Norval Glenn, Transformation of the Negro American (New York: Harper and Row, 1965), p. 9.

[23]Ibid.

[24]E. Franklin Frazier, The Negro Church in America (New York: Schocken Books, 1963), pp. 44-45.

[25]Ibid., pp. 42-44.

[26]Ibid., 31-42.

[27]Hudson, p. 220.

[28]Ibid., p. 222.

[29]Some schools formed were: Fisk, Atlanta and Tougaloo Universities, Talladega College and Hampton Institute (Ibid., p. 221).

[30]Reimers, p. 52.

[31]Ibid., p. 51.

[32]Thomas F. Gossett, Race: The History of an Idea in America (Dallas: Southern Methodist University Press, 1963), p. 193ff. Gossett has shown that Josiah Strong was not followed by clergymen in his zeal for the coming victories of the Anglo

Saxons, neither was he criticized for his racist theories. No clergymen of the period, it would appear, ever attacked him for his unfeeling attitude toward the rights of nonwhite races. "From those men from whom we might have expected criticism, such Social Gospel figures as Theodore Munger, Washington Gladden, Walter Rauschenbusch, Lyman Abbott, and George T. Herron, it was not forthcoming. . . . Though it is certainly unlikely that the other leaders of the movement shared Strong's ideas on race, one soon notices in their writings a timidity and a general discomfort in the area of racial theory or the rights of racial minorities."
[33]Reimers, pp. 54-55, italics ours.

Chapter 3: Christianity and Ghettoization
[1]Lerone Bennett, Jr., *Confrontation: Black and White* (Baltimore: Pelican Books, 1965).
[2]Silberman, p. 28. Cf. St. Clair Drake and Horace R. Cayton, *Black Metropolis: A Study of Negro Life in a Northern City*, rev. ed. (New York: Harper and Row, 1962), pp. 58-64.
[3]*Ibid.*
[4]Broom and Glenn, p. 164.
[5]*Ibid.*
[6]*Report of the National Advisory Commission on Civil Disorders*, pp. 217ff.
[7]*Ibid.*, p. 218.
[8]*Ibid.*, p. 219.
[9]*Ibid.*, p. 224.
[10]Franklin, *From Slavery to Freedom*, pp. 452-76, 573-600.
[11]Cf. Herbert Aptheker, *Negro Slave Revolts in the United States* (New York: International Publishers, 1939); and Joanne Grant, *Black Protest: History, Documents and Analyses, 1619 to the Present* (Greenwich, Conn.: Fawcett Publications, 1968).
[12]A discussion of these organizations and their philosophies is found in Kenneth B. Clark, "The Civil Rights Movement: Momentum and Organization," in *The Negro American*.
[13]Harold Baron, "The Web of Urban Racism" in *Institutional Racism in America*, ed. by Louis L. Knowles and Kenneth Prewitt (Englewood Cliffs, N.J.: Prentice-Hall, 1969), pp. 142-43.
[14]*Ibid.*
[15]Reimers, p. 87.
[16]*Ibid.*, p. 95.
[17]Frank S. Loescher, *The Protestant Church and the Negro* (New York: Association Press, 1948), p. 7.
[18]Mary Harrington Hall, "A Conversation with Kenneth B. Clark," *Psychology Today*, June 1968, p. 20.
[19]Gibson Winter, *The Suburban Captivity of the Churches* (New York: Macmillan, 1962), p. 50.
[20]Kardiner and Ovesey, p. 45.
[21]J. W. Johnson, *Along This Way* (New York: Viking Press, 1933), p. 170.
[22]Cf. Calvin Herton, *Sex and Racism in America* (New York: Grove Press, Inc., 1965); and Grier and Cobbs. The logical extension of this fear of interracial mixing is the

prohibition of interracial marriages. But there is no biblical basis to support such restrictions. The only biblical restriction on marriage is that a man marry a woman and a woman a man.

²³Eldridge Cleaver, *Soul on Ice* (New York: McGraw-Hill, 1968), p. 165. Cleaver, who has returned to the United States from self-imposed exile, has in the past professed conversion to Jesus Christ. This is expressed in his autobiographical book *Soul on Fire* (Waco, Tex.: Word, 1978). However, this is not to be viewed in any way as an invalidation of the statement which we have quoted from his earlier work.

²⁴Broom and Glenn, p. 13.
²⁵*Ibid.*
²⁶Frazier, p. 51.
²⁷Adam Clayton Powell, Jr., *Marching Blacks* (New York: Dial Press, 1945), 198-99.
²⁸Pierre Berton, *The Comfortable Pew* (Philadelphia: J. B. Lippincott, 1965), p. 29.
²⁹*Ibid.*, p. 31.
³⁰*Ibid.*
³¹James Baldwin, "How Can We Get the Black People to Cool It?" *Esquire*, July 1968, pp. 48ff.

Chapter 4: Glimpses of the New Identity
¹For more detailed discussions of these Black protesters see: Henry J. Young, *Major Black Religious Leaders: 1755-1940* (Nashville: Abingdon, 1977); and John Killinger, "Reaping the Whirlwind: God in the Literature of the Black Experience" in The Fragile Presence: Transcendence in Modern Literature (Philadelphia: Fortress, 1973).
²Leon F. Litwack, *North of Slavery: The Negro in the Free States, 1790-1860*, Phoenix Books (Chicago: Univ. of Chicago Press, 1961), p. 191.
³Bennett, p. 44, italics ours.
⁴*Ibid.*, p. 43.
⁵Herbert Aptheker, *Nat Turner's Slave Rebellion* (New York: Grove Press, Inc., 1966), p. 43.
⁶Quoted in Herbert Aptheker, *Nat Turner's Slave Rebellion*, p. 107.
⁷Litwack, p. 209.
⁸Carter G. Woodson, ed., *Negro Orators and Their Orations* (Washington, D.C.: Associated Publications, 1925), p. 215.
⁹James Cone, *The Spirituals and the Blues* (New York: Seabury Press, 1972), p. 35.
¹⁰*Ibid.*
¹¹Quoted in Reimers, p. 180.
¹²Langston Hughes, *Semple's Uncle Sam* (New York: Hill and Wang, 1968), p. 20, italics ours.
¹³*Ibid.*, pp. 95ff., italics ours.
¹⁴James Baldwin, *The Fire Next Time* (New York: Dell Publishing, 1968), p. 46, italics ours.
¹⁵Malcolm X, *Autobiography* (New York: Grove Press, 1965), pp. 24-42, italics ours.
¹⁶C. Eric Lincoln, *The Black Muslims in America* (Boston: Beacon Press, 1961), pp. 69-70.
¹⁷*Autobiography.*

Chapter 5: The Emergence of Black Consciousness

[1]W. E. Burghardt DuBois, The Souls of Black Folk (New York: Fawcett World Library, 1961), p. 75.

[2]Grier and Cobbs in Black Rage, pp. 50-62, analyze the survival style of Black Americans as expressed through the lives of Black women. Their conclusion is that any style of life which perpetuated human life under such dehumanizing conditions has to be an expression of good, normal human adjustment.

[3]Brewton Berry in Race and Ethnic Relations, 2nd ed. (Boston: Houghton Mifflin, 1958), p. 475ff. lists four different sets of patterns of adjustment to discrimination. His own consists of (1) acceptance, (2) avoidance, (3) assimilation and (4) aggression. The unique and revealing method employed by S. M. Strong in "Negro-white Relations as Reflected in Social Types," The American Journal of Sociology, 52 (July 1946), pp. 23-30, and recorded in Berry, pp. 468-69, uses the language employed by Blacks at that time: (1) the "white man's nigger" ("Uncle Tom"), (2) the "bad nigger," (3) the "smart nigger," (4) the "white man's strumpet," (5) the "mammy," (6) the "sheet lover," (7) the "race leader," (8) the "race man," (9) the "race woman." Thomas F. Pettigrew's A Profile of the Negro American (Princeton: D. Van Nostrand, 1964) and Abram Kardiner's and Lionel Ovesey's The Mark of Oppression: Explorations in the Personality of the American Negro (Cleveland: World Publishing, 1951) should also be seen for more information on this point.

[4]It is very likely that any one black-skinned American can exhibit characteristics of all three psychological types—Black, Negro or "street nigger"—in response to the White world. These categories should not be understood as being unchangeable. Thus many Negroes and "street niggers" are in "transition" toward Black.

The viability and potentiality of the Black consciousness movement is directly proportional to the ability of Blacks to establish a working rapport with "street niggers." This working rapport maintains the pressure on White society (and Negroes) to recognize the legitimacy of the Black protest.

[5]Stokely Carmichael and Charles V. Hamilton, Black Power: The Politics of Liberation in America (New York: Random, Vintage Books, 1967), pp. 37-38.

[6]Fyodor Dostoyevsky, The Brothers Karamazov, trans. by Constance Garnett (New York: New American Library, 1957), p. 238, italics ours.

[7]James Baldwin, Nobody Knows My Name (New York: Dell Publishing, 1963), p. 38, italics ours.

[8]Carmichael and Hamilton, p. 47.

[9]Tannenbaum, p. 115.

[10]Julius Lester, Black Folktales (New York: Richard W. Baron, 1969), p. 130.

[11]See C. Eric Lincoln, The Black Muslims in America (Boston: Beacon Press, 1961); E. U. Essien-Udom, Black Nationalism: A Search for an Identity in America (New York: Dell Publishing, 1964); and Louis E. Lomax, When the World Is Given (Cleveland: World Publishing, 1963). The reader should also note that Black Theology in its early manifestation was developed by Marcus Garvey in the 1920s. See Marcus Garvey, Philosophy of Opinions of Marcus Garvey, 2 vols. (New York: Univ. Publishing House, 1923) and E. D. Cronon, Black Moses (Madison: Univ. of Wisconsin Press, 1962).

[12]Since the death of the Honorable Elijah Muhammad in 1975, his son Imman Wallace D. Muhammad has changed the emphasis of this Movement. Called "The

American Muslim Mission," it is closely aligned with orthodox Islam and has a strong religious emphasis, as opposed to the previous emphasis on socio-economic change.

[13]Louis E. Lomax, *The Negro Revolt* (New York: New American Library, 1962), p. 188.

[14]*Ibid.*

[15]See his *Black Messiah* (New York: Sheed and Ward, 1968).

[16]Quoted in an important and widely circulated article: "The Quest for a Black Christ," *Ebony*, March 1969, p. 174.

[17]*Ibid.*, p. 176.

[18]James H. Cone, *A Black Theology of Liberation* (Philadelphia: Lippincott, 1970), p. 24.

[19]*Ibid.*, p. 25.

[20]The definitive source for the study of Black Theology as it developed in the '70s is: *Black Theology: A Documentary History, 1966-1979*, ed. by Gayraud Wilmore and James Cone. Cone's later works are also important: *The Spirituals and the Blues* and *God of the Oppressed*. Also of interest are the works by Major J. Jones, Henry Mitchell and J. Deotis Roberts. See the bibliography for more information.

Chapter 6: What Blacks Must Know about Christianity

[1]Frederick Douglass, *Narrative of the Life of Frederick Douglass: An American Slave*, Signet Books (New York: New American Library, 1968), p. 120.

[2]Malcolm X, p. 286.

[3]Silberman, p. 174. We do not feel that it is wise to speculate upon Canaan's impropriety, yet the fact remains that Canaan, not Ham, was both the "guilty" and the "cursed" individual.

[4]William F. Albright, "The Old Testament World," *The Interpreter's Bible* (New York: Abingdon Press, 1952), I, 270.

[5]Gen 10:6-14. DuBois in *The World and Africa*, chaps. 5-6, corroborates the *Black*-*ness* of these ancient kingdoms. See also J. C. deGraft-Johnson, *African Glory* (New York: Walker and Company, 1954); Harry R. Hall, *Ancient History of the Near East*, 11th ed. (New York: Barnes and Noble, 1960); and Harry R. Johnston, *A History of the Colonization of Africa by Alien Races* (New York: Cooper Square, 1966).

[6]Consider Jacob and his two wives, Leah and Rachel, the actions of Israel in conquering Canaan and the bill of divorcement provision in Deuteronomy 24:1-4.

[7]Cf. Tit 2:9-10; Eph 6:5-9; Col 3:22-25; 1 Pet 2:18-25; and 1 Tim 6:1-2.

[8]Cf. William L. Westermann, *Slave Systems of Greek and Roman Antiquity* (Philadelphia: American Philosophical Society, 1955). The reader is also encouraged to compare the similarities between Latin American and Roman slavery, both of which contrast with slavery in the United States. See Tannenbaum, *passim*.

[9]*Ibid.*

[10]Col 4:1 (KJV).

[11]Stuart Barton Babbage, *Man in Nature and in Grace* (Grand Rapids: Eerdmans, 1957), p. 11.

[12]Leona E. Tyler, *The Psychology of Human Differences*, 3rd ed. (New York: Appleton-Century-Crofts, 1965), p. 304.

[13]Quoted in Edmund Fuller, *Affirmations of God and Man: Writings for Modern*

Dialogue (New York: Association Press, 1967), pp. 48-49.

[14]Leon Morris, *The Lord from Heaven: A Study of the New Testament Teaching on the Deity and Humanity of Jesus Christ* (Grand Rapids: Eerdmans, 1958), p. 45.

[15]Paul Ramsey, *Basic Christian Ethics* (New York: Charles Scribner's Sons, 1950), pp. 92ff.

[16]The color of Jesus in our thinking is totally irrelevant to that which he came to accomplish and that which he demonstrated. We do not find in his life any attitudes which would suggest that a person must give up his Blackness or Whiteness in order to become a Christian. If one wants to consider the color of Jesus using racist criteria (i.e., "one drop of Black blood makes you Black"), then Jesus *is* Black.

[17]See, for example, 1 Corinthians 6:9-11; James 2:1-7; Acts 16:25-34.

Chapter 7: What White Christians Must Do with Their Churches

[1]Lewis M. Killian, *The Impossible Revolution? Black Power and the American Dream* (New York: Random House, 1968), p. 23.

[2]Peter Berger, *The Noise of Solemn Assemblies* (New York: Doubleday, 1961), p. 116.

[3]Richard Wright, *White Man, Listen!* (New York: Doubleday, 1964), p. xvi, italics ours.

[4]*Report of the National Advisory Commission on Civil Disorders*, p. 2.

[5]Cf. Paul's statements in 1 Timothy 4:1 and 6:11 in which Timothy is exhorted to work for righteousness despite growing evil.

[6]The case for God's interest in justice is well made in *Cry Justice*, ed. Ronald J. Sider (Downers Grove, Ill.: InterVarsity Press, 1980).

[7]John R. Roche and Milton M. Gordon, "Can Morality Be Legislated?" in *American Minorities: A Textbook of Readings in Intergroup Relations*, ed. by Milton L. Barron (New York: Alfred A. Knopf, 1958), pp. 490-96. These authors conclude that although local considerations may call for special forms of implementation, "the majesty of law, when supported by the collective conscience of a people and the healing power of the social situation, in the long run will not only enforce morality but create it"(p. 496).

[8]David O. Moberg, *Inasmuch: Christian Social Responsibility in 20th Century America* (Grand Rapids: Eerdmans, 1965), p. 14.

[9]*Ibid.*

[10]In past decades several White evangelicals have come to agree with the position stated here concerning the twin Christian duties of evangelism and social action. See, for example, *Christian Mission in the Modern World* (1975) by John R. W. Stott; *The New Face of Evangelicalism* (1976) by C. René Padilla (an analysis of the significant 1974 Lausanne conference); *God's People in God's World: Biblical Motives for Social Involvement* (1979) by John Gladwin, all published by Inter-Varsity Press. Two magazines evidencing this trend are *Sojourners* (1309 L St. NW, Washington, DC 20005) and *The Other Side* (300 W. Apsley, Philadelphia, PA 19144). Both of these publications are produced by communities of people committed to the amelioration of racial discrimination in our society.

[11]Samples and price lists for materials may be requested from: Urban Ministries, Inc., 9917 Green St., Chicago, IL 60643. Samples are available for free to pastors or Sunday-school superintendents only.

[12]For information write: Voice of Calvary Ministries, 1655 St. Charles St., Jackson, MI 39209.

Selected Bibliography

Black History

Bennett, Lerone, Jr. *Before the Mayflower: A History of the Negro in America, 1619-1964.* New York: Penguin Books, 1964.

Franklin, John Hope. *From Slavery to Freedom: A History of American Negroes.* 5th ed. New York: Alfred A. Knopf, 1978.

Sherer, Lester B. *Slavery and the Churches in Early America, 1619-1819.* Grand Rapids: Eerdmans, 1975.

Young, Henry J. *Major Black Religious Leaders: 1755-1940.* Nashville: Abingdon, 1977.

Black Theology

Cone, James H. *A Black Theology of Liberation.* New York: Lippincott, 1970.

_____. *Black Theology and Black Power.* New York: Seabury Press, 1969.

_____. *God of the Oppressed.* New York: Seabury Press, 1975.

_____. *The Spirituals and the Blues.* New York: Seabury Press, 1972.

Frazier, E. Franklin and Lincoln, C. Eric. *The Negro Church in America and the Black Church since Frazier.* New York: Schocken Books, 1974.

Hamilton, Charles V. *The Black Preacher in America.* New York: William Morrow, 1972.

Jones, Major J. *Black Awareness: A Theology of Hope.* Nashville: Abingdon, 1971.

_____. *Christian Ethics for Black Theology.* Nashville: Abingdon, 1974.

Lincoln, C. Eric, ed. *The Black Experience in Religion.* Garden City: Doubleday, 1974.

Mitchell, Henry. *Black Belief.* New York: Harper & Row, 1975.

_____. *Black Preaching*. New York: Harper & Row, 1979.

Roberts, J. Deotis. *A Black Political Theology*. Philadelphia: Westminster Press, 1974.

_____. *Liberation and Reconciliation: A Black Theology*. Philadelphia: Westminster Press, 1971.

Wilmore, Gayraud S. *Black Religion and Black Radicalism*. New York: Doubleday, 1972.

Wilmore, Gayraud and Cone, James H., eds. *Black Theology: A Documentary History, 1966-1979*. Maryknoll, N.Y.: Orbis Books, 1979.

Books by Black Evangelicals

Banks, William. *The Black Church in the U.S.* Chicago: Moody Press, 1972.

Bentley, William H. *The Meaning of History for Black Americans*. NBEA & NBCSC (P.O. Box 4311, Chicago, Ill. 60680), 1979.

_____. *National Black Evangelical Association: Evolution of a Concept of Ministry*. Rev. ed. Chicago: NBEA, 1979.

_____. *The Relevance of a Black Evangelical Theology for American Theology*. Chicago: BECN, 1981.

Evans, Anthony. *Biblical Theology and the Black Experience*. Dallas: Black Evangelistic Enterprise, 1977.

Perkins, John. *Let Justice Roll Down*. Glendale, Calif.: Regal Books, 1976.

_____. *A Quiet Revolution*. Waco, Tex.: Word Books, 1976.

Skinner, Tom. *How Black Is the Gospel?* New York: Lippincott, 1970.

Books to Sensitize Whites

Barndt, Joseph. *Liberating Our White Ghetto*. Minneapolis: Augsburg, 1972.

Brown, Claude. *Manchild in the Promised Land*. New York: Macmillan, 1965.

Cleaver, Eldridge. *Soul on Fire*. Waco, Tex.: Word Books, 1978.

_____. *Soul on Ice*. New York: Dell Publishing, Delta Books, 1968.

Haley, Alex. *The Autobiography of Malcolm X*. New York: Grove Press, 1965.

_____. *Roots: The Saga of an American Family*. New York: Dell, 1976.

Shockley, Donald G. *Free, White and Christian*. Nashville: Abingdon, 1975.

Terry, Robert W. *For Whites Only*. Grand Rapids, Mich.: Eerdmans, 1970.

Wright, Nathan, Jr. *Let's Face Racism*. Camden, N. J.: T. Nelson, 1970.

Wright, Richard. *Native Son*. New York: Harper & Row, 1940.

Index